JOE ORTON

Loot

with commentary and notes by
ANDREW MAYNE

METHUEN DRAMA

Methuen Student Edition

10 9 8 7 6 5 4 3 2 1

This edition first published in Great Britain in 1985
by Methuen London Ltd
Reissued with a new cover design and additional material in 2006

Methuen Drama
A & C Black Publishers Limited
38 Soho Square
London W1D 3HB

Loot first published by Methuen and Co. Ltd in 1967
Copyright © 1967 by the Estate of Joe Orton

Commentary and Notes copyright © 1985, 2006 by Methuen London Ltd

The rights of Joe Orton and Andrew Mayne to be identified respectively
as the author of the play and the author of the commentary and notes
have been asserted by them in accordance with the Copyright, Designs
and Patents Act, 1988

A CIP catalogue record for this book is available from the British Library

ISBN 0-413-56760-5
    978-0-413-56760-4

Set by Tek-Art, Croydon, Surrey
Printed in Great Britain by Bookmarque Ltd, Croydon, Surrey

*Thanks are due to Chris Johnson and to Elizabeth Mayne for their
helpful comments in the preparation of the Commentary to this edition*

Contents

Joe Orton: a brief life

    Early career – and influences   v

    A spell inside – and dramatic achievement   vii

    Orton's diaries – and his death   x

Plot   xii

Commentary

    The play's genre   xvi

    Characterization   xix

    Language and humour   xxv

    Critical differences   xxxii

Further reading   xxxvii

LOOT   5

Notes   89

Questions for further study   100

Between page xxxvii and the play text is a selection of photos by Donald Cooper from the 1984 production at the Ambassadors Theatre directed by Jonathan Lynn with Leonard Rossiter as Truscott

Joe Orton: a brief life

Early career — and influences

John Kingsley Orton was born on 1 January 1933, the eldest of four children, and brought up on the Saffron Lane Estates in Leicester, an industrial city in the Midlands. His mother, Elsie, worked first as a machinist in a hosiery factory and then, as her eyesight failed, as a charwoman; his hen-pecked father, William, was a gardener with the Leicester Council. Life in the Orton family's council house was both emotionally and materially rather impoverished. As a child Orton suffered from asthma which meant frequent absences from school. When he failed the Eleven-Plus examination for entry into Grammar School, his mother, who always favoured John as the most gifted of her children, scraped together the fees to send him to Clark's College, a private school which in its emphasis on commercial training was probably not the right environment for Orton. At school Orton was found to be barely literate, though later he was to embark on a programme of considerable self-education. After leaving school at sixteen he never held a job for very long — 'I was sacked from all the jobs I had between sixteen and eighteen because I was never interested in any of them' — and he turned to amateur dramatics for the promise of fulfilment which his home and working environment failed to provide.

After taking elocution lessons with a view to eradicating his lisp and local accent, Orton gained a place in 1950 at RADA (The Royal Academy of Dramatic Art) and the support of a Leicester Council Grant. Orton was later disparaging — 'I didn't have a very good time at RADA . . . I was more enthusiastic and knew more about acting at the beginning of my first term than I did at the end' — but it was at RADA that he met Kenneth Halliwell who was to have a decisive influence on his later life. Halliwell was seven years his elder and he was able to provide both the literary knowledge and the independent financial means which Orton lacked. A month after Orton arrived in London, he moved into Halliwell's flat; their homosexual relationship, though latterly it was to undergo severe strains, lasted until the end.

In 1953, after leaving RADA, Orton was assistant stage manager at a provincial repertory theatre (Ipswich) for four months, but it was not an experience he enjoyed and he was soon back in London with Halliwell. Halliwell had inspired Orton with the ambition to write and they isolated themselves in their Islington bedsitting room, at first working on joint enterprises, writing novels strongly flavoured by the influence of Ronald Firbank.

Ronald Firbank (1866-1926) has had an influence on a number of twentieth-century writers which may seem out of proportion to the slight and eccentric nature of his work. He presents the reader with a rarefied world, devoid of values, in which the only virtues are the cultivation of an aestheticism − by means of a prose style which is both fastidious and fantastic − and the maintenance of a detached level of witty (and sometimes sniggering) sophistication. Firbank's narrative technique is spare, and dialogue is always very prominent in novels such as *Valmouth* (1919) and *The Eccentricities of Cardinal Pirelli* (1926) − a story in which the hero meets his end while pursuing a choir-boy round the altar. The pervasive tone is one of stylish 'camp' decadence − to be shared with a coterie readership. To Orton Firbank's appeal was partly stylistic: he demonstrated some of the effects that could be achieved in prose through a careful shaping of sentences. Just as importantly, however, his perverse delight in the apparently trivial utterance beneath which, to the initiated, lurks depravity, provided Orton with what was to become a keynote of his own work. No doubt Orton was also fascinated by Firbank's elegant blending of the exotic and the vulgar, a quality which may be sampled in the following extract from *Valmouth*. It describes Mrs Thoroughfare at her devotions in the ornate chapel of Hare-Hatch House:

> Beyond a perpetual vigil-lamp or two the Basilica was unlit.
> Glancing nervously at the unostentatious (essentially unostentatious) font, Mrs Thoroughfare swept softly over a milky-blue porcelain floor (slightly slithery to the feet) to where her pet prie-dieu, laden with pious provender like some good mountain mule, stood waiting, ready for her to mount, which with a short sigh she did.
> 'Teach me to know myself, O Lord. Show me my heart. Help me to endure,' she prayed, addressing a figurine in purple and white faience by Maurice Denis below the *quête*.
> Through the interstices of the be-pillared nave (brilliant with a series of Gothic banners) the sunlight teemed, illuminating the

numerous *ex-votos*, and an esoteric little altar-piece of the
'School' of Sodoma.

   'O grant me force!' she murmured, unbending a shade at
sight of the gala altar-cloth where, crumpled up amid paschal
lilies and *fleurs-de-luce*, basked an elaborate frizzed lamb of her
own devoted working . . .

   'Hail, Mary . . .!' she breathed, ignoring a decanter of sherry
and a plate of herring-sandwiches — a contrivance akin to genius
in drawing attention to an offertory-box near by.

   From the sacristy the refined roulades of a footman (these
'satanic' matches!) reached her faintly:

      'Oh I'm his gala-gairlie . . .

   I'm his gala child,

   Yes,' etc.

   Useless, under the circumstances, to attempt a *station*!

Though an unbeliever himself, Firbank rejoiced in the satiric
possibilities of Catholic observance. In *Loot* Orton was to tune to
this same wavelength and some crackles of Firbank remain in the
background. Like most writers who are learning their craft, Orton
was good at absorbing influences, but at this earlier stage of his
career, the influence of Firbank was probably too pervasive.
Halliwell had guided him to Firbank. Temperamentally Orton
shared Firbank's nihilistic views and was perhaps attracted by the
possibility of raising his own linguistic gifts to the level at which
Firbank's defence against the darkness — a glittering stylistic
firework display — might be possible; but there was too much of
Firbank in the novels Orton wrote with Halliwell and could not get
published — they had titles such as *The Mechanical Womb* and *The
Last Days of Sodom*. Maybe Orton felt the need to push Halliwell's
own literary influence a little to one side. The writing partnership
which Halliwell had once dominated was coming to an end. After
1957 Orton was producing mainly work of his own, though it was
to take another half-dozen years before he discovered his own
authentic voice.

A spell inside — and dramatic achievement

Their claustrophobic existence came to a crisis in May 1962 when
Orton and Halliwell were charged with maliciously damaging 83
books and removing 1,653 illustrations from library books. Since
1959, with Halliwell's help, Orton had been stealing books from
public libraries, removing the pictures and using them to make up

bizarre collages, composed by Halliwell, which covered the walls of their bedsitter. The activity was essentially a subversive practical joke and a kind of puerile retribution aimed at a literary world which excluded Orton, despite, as Orton said, 'all the rubbish that was being published'. Orton went to considerable pains in his acts of defacement:

> I did things like pasting a picture of a female nude over a book of etiquette, over the picture of the author who, I think, was Lady Lewisham. I did other things, very strange things . . . I used to write false blurbs on the inside of Gollancz books because I discovered that Gollancz books had blank yellow flaps and I used to type false blurbs on the insides. My blurbs were mildly obscene. Even at the trial they said they were only mildly obscene. When I put the plastic covers back over the jackets you couldn't tell that the blurbs weren't printed. I used to stand in corners after I'd smuggled the doctored books back into the library and then watch people read them. It was very funny, very interesting. There was a biography of Sybil Thorndike in which there was a picture of her locked up in a cell as Nurse Edith Cavell. I cut the caption from another picture and pasted it under the picture, so that it read: 'During the war I received many strange requests'. One of the interesting things at the trial was that the greatest outrage, the one for which I think I was sent to prison, was that I had stuck a monkey's face in the middle of a rose, on the cover of something called Collins' *Book of Roses*. It was a very beautiful yellow rose. What I had done was held as the depth of iniquity for which I should probably have been birched. They won't ever do that so they just sent me to prison for six months.

Prison confirmed Orton's views about English society — 'The old whore society lifted up her skirts, and the stench was pretty foul' — but in some ways the experience may have helped: 'Being in the nick,' Orton observed, 'brought detachment to my writing. I wasn't involved any more and it suddenly worked'. Within a year of his release the BBC had accepted the radio version of his play *The Ruffian on the Stair*, and he had started work on a full-length play, *Entertaining Mr Sloane*, which opened in May 1964 at the New Arts Theatre and was soon transferred to the West End. It was a controversial success. On the one hand, Rattigan, the master of the 'well-made play' praised *Entertaining Mr Sloane* as 'the best first play' he had seen 'in thirty odd years'; on the other, many were outraged by the way the playwright neatly side-stepped conventional morality. The play shows us how the apparently amoral and bisexual Sloane initially plays off against each other a brother and sister who are both eager to compete for Sloane's sexual favour; but the tables are finally turned on Sloane when, after he has killed their father, the brother and sister establish their joint proprietorial rights over him and agree to share his body on a rota basis. Orton gleefully stoked the fires of the *succès de scandale* which the play produced by writing to the *Daily Telegraph* under the pseudonym of Edna Welthorpe (Mrs): 'I myself was nauseated by this endless parade of mental and physical perversion. And to be told that such a disgusting piece of filth now passes for humour.'

In 1964 Orton also wrote *The Good and Faithful Servant* (televised 1967) which signalled a move towards black comedy in its portrayal of a worker, Buchanan, thrown onto the scrapheap after fifty years' service for one firm. The play adopts a fiercely anti-authoritarian stance, and to some extent it prepares the way for the writing of *Loot* which was completed in its first version in October 1964, though in the later play farce provides a frame for the iconoclastic humour. It was planned to prepare for a West End run of *Loot* with a short provincial tour, but despite a very strong cast (Kenneth Williams, Geraldine McEwen, Ian McShane, Duncan Macrae), the production ran into serious difficulties which entailed constant rewriting by Orton as the play was on the road. (The story of the play's difficult birth may be found in chapter 5 of John Lahr's biography of Orton, *Prick Up Your Ears*.) Having opened in February 1965 at Cambridge, this first production of *Loot* failed and folded at Wimbledon in March. No West End management would accept the play. Dismayed by this reverse, Orton produced only one play in 1965 — *The Erpingham Camp*, a television drama set in a holiday camp which has a deranged dictator at its head who faces an inept uprising from revolutionary holiday-makers. *Loot* was, however, staged with some success in April 1966 at the University Theatre, Manchester, after Orton had again substantially modified the play, as he would keep on doing right up to the time of its eventual appearance in London that September. This production, directed by Charles Marowitz, received awards from both the *Evening Standard* and from *Plays and Players* as the best play of 1966 and Orton was encouraged to embark on a most productive period of writing which spanned the period from October 1966 to his death in August of the following year.

He wrote *Funeral Games*, a script for television, which reworks almost to exhaustion that vein, present in *Loot*, of anti-Christian satire; he dashed off a film script, *Up Against It*, originally commissioned for the Beatles, though it remained unfilmed. (Orton had also sold the film rights of *Loot* for a substantial sum, though he confided to his diary that '*Loot* is quite unsuitable for filming', a judgment which the resulting film amply confirmed.) In this same period Orton was at work revising *The Erpingham Camp* and his first play, *The Ruffian on the Stair*, which early in 1967 was presented as a double-bill by the Royal Court under the title *Crimes of Passion*; and he completed his final full-length play, *What the Butler Saw* (produced posthumously in March 1969).

Orton's diaries — and his death

At this busy time, in the pleasing aftermath of *Loot*'s success, Orton had also resumed writing a diary, somthing he had once done as a schoolboy and a young man in his Leicester days. Even allowing for the inevitable element of narcissism inherent in any writing of this kind, these diaries reveal a coldly self-absorbed personality. It is not that Orton spends much time on the analysis of his own feelings; and rarely does he theorise or comment in any depth on the nature of his own artistic work. What seems to concern him most in the diaries is his own rise to success and affluence and the surface glitter — or tarnish — of life, particularly as it is manifested in gossip. Orton clearly loved gossip about the theatrical celebrities and showbiz figures with whom he was increasingly coming into contact — the more scurrilous it was, the more he enjoyed it. The diaries are also notable for the account they give of Orton's homosexual life. These promiscuous encounters are recorded in a whole series of action replays which detail who did what to whom, yet in terms of feeling they do little more than act out the advice Orton gave to a friend: 'Reject all the values of society. And enjoy sex. When you're dead you'll regret not having fun with your genital organs'.

The diaries do, however, shed light on the painful last period of Orton's relationship with Halliwell. In the early days of their association Halliwell had been the dominating partner. It had been Halliwell, who himself burned with a desire to be an artist, who had helped to bring Orton to a level at which artistic achievement was possible; but from the time of the success of *Entertaining Mr Sloane*, it was the former master who was obliged to watch from the sidelines, while the pupil received all the plaudits. It seemed to Halliwell that Orton did not wish to acknowledge in public the part the 'master' had played. Orton was increasingly moving in a world in which showbiz celebrities mingled with the wealthy and those blessed to play a part in the meretriciously 'swinging sixties'. It was a world in which Halliwell was often made to feel he was merely an appendage to his successful friend, or even a derided 'middle-aged nonentity'. Moreover, while Halliwell craved the dependency of a loving relationship, Orton insisted on giving full rein to his predatory and promiscuous homosexuality. Halliwell, possessive and vulnerable, alternating between ineffectual introspection and ridiculous self-assertion, grew neurotically ill. As Halliwell neared nervous breakdown, his sterile bickering with Orton increased, and despite Halliwell's repeated threats of suicide, Orton was clearly considering severing their relationship. John Lahr comments: 'In his sickness Halliwell, who needed love and said so, became increasingly unlovable . . . The more ferociously Halliwell clung to Orton, the more Orton felt the need to put distance between them'. The relationship of fifteen years came to an end in their Islington bedsitting room on 9 August 1967, when Halliwell murdered Orton by bludgeoning him over the head with a hammer; he then committed suicide by taking an overdose of sleeping tablets. Lahr provides an epitaph: 'Through murder Halliwell achieved the public association with Joe Orton's career he'd been denied in life'.

Plot

'To summarize in any detail the plot of a farce would be an act of singular madness.' (A. Enyam: *The Parameters of Farce*)

Act One

The action of the play opens in the lounge of Mr McLeavy's house on the afternoon of the funeral of McLeavy's wife. The predatory Fay, who has 'nursed' Mrs McLeavy during her illness, is eager to persuade the new widower to marry her post-haste. A wardrobe door in the room proves to be locked; Hal, McLeavy's son, refuses to open it, for we will soon learn that the cupboard contains the loot from a robbery carried out by Hal and his homosexual friend, Dennis; they have broken into a bank from the adjacent undertaker's premises where Dennis is employed. When Dennis arrives — he is driving the car which will bear Mrs McLeavy's body to the funeral — he tells Hal that the police are already on their trail. So, at Hal's suggestion, they transfer the stolen banknotes to the coffin and bundle the corpse upside-down into the wardrobe.

Truscott, a police inspector masquerading as an official of the metropolitan water board, arrives in the McLeavy household to conduct his investigations into the bank robbery: he finds out that the wardrobe door has suspiciously been kept locked by Hal; he reveals to Fay that he has discovered her intention of embarking on what will be her eighth marriage — evidently all of her previous husbands have met with violent and untimely deaths; and he elicits from Fay a specimen of her handwriting.

Fay discloses to McLeavy that, just before her death, his wife changed her will, leaving virtually all her estate to Fay. After his initial outrage and the expression of some doubts ('But then you'd have my money as well as Mrs McLeavy's'), McLeavy is on the point of yielding to Fay's requests and proposing marriage when the imminent departure of the funeral cortège interrupts him. Dennis, who has already had a sexual liaison with Fay, is upset to hear of her intention to marry McLeavy; Hal presses his friend's superior marital claims, stressing Dennis's new affluence: 'He's richer than my dad, you know'. Fay, her interest obviously aroused, absents herself from the funeral — as Hal has done already — and as a result of Hal's unfortunate inability to lie she soon discovers all about the switching of the loot and the corpse. After bargaining for a favourable share of the spoils, Fay agrees to undress the corpse behind a screen in preparation for dumping the body in the countryside.

Truscott's return causes a moment of frenzied activity as Fay and Hal attempt to hide the evidence of what they have been up to: Fay quickly pulls the screen around the bed on which the corpse lies, now swathed in bandages. Although Truscott is puzzled to find that there is nothing incriminating in the wardrobe, on discovering what is in fact the corpse he seems happy enough to accept Fay's explanation that the object is a tailor's dummy and he proceeds with his investigation into the bank robbery. In an attempt to force a confession of the whereabouts of the stolen money he beats and kicks Hal but will not accept Hal's statement that the loot is now 'in church'.

The beating up is interrupted by the surprising return of a shocked and heavily-bandaged McLeavy, who faints onto the bed just as Hal removes the corpse and shoves it behind the screen. McLeavy reports that the funeral cortège has met with a bad road accident: there has been one fatality, but evidently Dennis has bravely managed to rescue the coffin from the blazing car; subsequently McLeavy was savaged by an Afghan hound. When Dennis and Hal bring the charred coffin back into the room, the side falls away and Dennis has to shield the banknotes from the eyes of McLeavy and Truscott.

In the absence of McLeavy and Truscott, Dennis learns that Fay is now a partner in crime and as there is a possibility McLeavy may ask for the coffin to be re-opened, the trio begin to remove the banknotes while Dennis proposes marriage to Fay. They are interrupted, however, by the return of McLeavy, and the corpse cannot be hidden in time. McLeavy shrieks with horror when he sees it, but readily accepts Fay's explanation that the object is an 'appliance' that she uses when sewing vestments and altar cloths. McLeavy, once so complacently secure in the belief that the authorities and the police know best, is now considerably annoyed by the high-handed treatment he has received from Truscott.

Truscott enters and insists on questioning Dennis alone. The corpse is under the inspector's very nose, but he is only concerned first to browbeat Dennis on the subject of the young man's sexual licence and then to attempt once more to ascertain where the loot is hidden; both inveigling and violence fail to produce any positive information. Bad-temperedly Truscott instructs Dennis to leave and to take the 'sewing dummy' with him. However, just before the interval curtain falls the blundering police inspector does finally discover a clue. Now alone on stage, Truscott picks up and examines carefully a small object. It is, in fact, the glass eye which earlier had fallen from the corpse while Fay and Hal were carrying the body from the wardrobe to the bed.

Act Two
The Second Act begins with a neat device which suggests that there has been no gap in time in the action on stage: Truscott is still examining the glass eye under his pocket magnifying-glass. He is responding to McLeavy's bemused grievances when Dennis and Hal break into the room carrying the corpse which, of course, Truscott still believes to be a tailor's dummy.

With some pride Truscott now reveals his true identity as a police inspector of considerable repute, and he declares that, beginning with a case of murder, he will now bring to light the crimes he has been investigating. He side-steps Fay's desperate claim that Mrs McLeavy has spoken to her from beyond the grave to accuse her husband of murder and, referring to a book on the trial of Phyllis McMahon (one of his own former cases), he produces the specimen of Fay's handwriting to identify her as both the murderer in this earlier case and the killer of Mrs McLeavy. He informs McLeavy of his lucky escape and forces a confession of guilt from Fay. Fay is arrested and Truscott believes all that is now required for a conviction is a post-mortem examination, which will establish precisely the cause of Mrs McLeavy's death. However, when Truscott learns from Dennis that the casket which contained the contents of Mrs McLeavy's stomach has been destroyed in the motor accident, the police inspector is forced to marvel that once again providence seems to have ensured a last-minute reprieve for Fay; though it may still be possible, he feels, to charge Fay as an accessory to robbery.

At this point Truscott produces the glass eye; he requires that it be returned to its 'rightful owner' and orders the dummy to be unwrapped. McLeavy has, however, recognized that the true origin of the glass eye is the embalmed corpse of his wife, and he is outraged by the idea that Hal has stolen this item. Fearing further acts of theft he insists that the coffin should be opened, and this he does himself, against the advice (for different reasons) of both

Truscott and the criminal trio. McLeavy is horrified when he discovers the loot in the coffin and he sinks beside the bandaged corpse in a state of shock; Truscott accepts Fay's explanation of McLeavy's reaction — the corpse has deteriorated badly, she says — and is disinclined to examine the contents of the coffin for himself.

The enormity of his son's crimes having been revealed to him, McLeavy is obviously at first determined to prefer charges, despite the pleas of all three criminals; but faced with the dilemma of having to betray his son, he finally relents and, going against the grain of his character, he lies to Truscott: he was wrong to claim that the glass eye belonged to his wife's corpse. Fay gladly confirms that Truscott's original deduction that the eye came from her sewing dummy was correct. Truscott now threatens to have his men turn the whole house upside-down in a search for the stolen money; he himself will return shortly to take possession of the remains of Mrs McLeavy.

While McLeavy goes off to confess his sins to his priest, Fay, Dennis and Hal decide that they will be safe from detection if they unwrap the corpse, replace it in the coffin and then stash the loot in the casket which formerly contained the contents of Mrs McLeavy's stomach and which Truscott will not bother to search because he believes it to be empty; but when Truscott returns he does, in fact, require the casket — it must be 'certified empty'; its lid swings open and banknotes scatter at Truscott's feet.

McLeavy seems almost pleased that the criminals' guilt has now been revealed, but Hal's prompt offer of a substantial bribe is accepted by Truscott and the spoils from the robbery are amicably divided between the three criminals and the police inspector. After McLeavy objects and threatens to expose what has just taken place, Truscott, at Hal's suggestion, agrees that the solution will be to arrest McLeavy who is taken away protesting his innocence. It is suggested that an 'accidental death' can be arranged for McLeavy while he is in custody.

Hal, Dennis and Fay are left feeling well-disposed towards Truscott. Fay will marry Dennis and she quickly establishes her proprietorial rights over him.

Commentary

The design of farce and its moral assumptions
The plot of *Loot* is full of intricate twists and turns, improbable
events and bizarre situations. These are the basic ingredients of
farce, a type of drama which celebrates the principle that, if in life
things can go wrong, they will — again and again. The story-line of
a farce is like an obstacle course in which characters have to
surmount barriers of ever-increasing difficulty and complexity,
these barriers taking such forms as the swift juxtaposition of
coincidences, misunderstandings, confusions and mistaken
identities. The action is fast and frenetic and moves through crisis
and mayhem towards threatening castastrophe; though in a
conventional farce a highly-organized plot, which will often show
strong elements of symmetry, finally heads off disaster and ensures
a happy resolution — for we know throughout that we are in an
exaggerated world of comic artifice.

Much of the comedy in farce is visual and the surprise entry is
its stock-in-trade — as we see in *Loot* when the heavily bandaged
McLeavy makes his dramatic entry after the motor accident (p.48).
Characters will often make a series of quick entrances and exits
which are carefully orchestrated by the dramatist to produce
maximum discomfiture for any character who wishes to hide some
guilty secret or avoid some embarrassing encounter. Orton uses this
device many times in *Loot* as we witness the frenzied shuttling
around of Mrs McLeavy's body and the loot in order to avoid
detection by Truscott or discovery by Mr McLeavy. The audience
is made to anticipate the imminency of the arrival of one of these
two characters by the falling of a shadow on the glass panel of the
lounge door, and in *Loot* the cream of the jest is that detection and
discovery are delayed to an extreme degree because of Truscott's
elaborate stupidity and McLeavy's excessive gullibility. In a
travesty of the hackneyed detective drama, the Whodunit, Truscott
repeatedly fails to recognize the most incriminating evidence of
murder, even when such evidence is under his very nose. The play

is full of outrageous situations which are apparently regarded by the characters as being quite normal and improbable explanations which are readily credited. Note, for instance, the parallel cases of both Truscott's and McLeavy's acceptance of Fay's story about her sewing dummy (pp.44 and 54).

In farce the most unlikely explanation frequently determines the action, and the characters are powerlessly caught up in a series of events which, like some machine out of control, hurtles them towards catastrophe. In Orton's hands, this becomes a kind of metaphor for the world he believes we inhabit; it is a mad world, or it will at least appear so, Orton insists, if we expect it to conform to rational explanation. *Loot*, as we shall see in greater detail later, shows a reworking of the normal pattern of farce: far from returning us, after all the complications, safe and sound to an ordered world, the play moves inevitably towards a reversal of our conventional expectations.

This is not what English farce generally provides: in England, farce has customarily been regarded as a congenial form of popular entertainment. The French variety, as produced by Feydeau for instance (see *La Puce à l'oreille*, 1907, translated as *A Flea in Her Ear*), may once have been regarded as rather 'naughty' because of the permissive latitude given to the portrayal of sexual behaviour; but the English product, though full of *double-entendre*, offers a sanitized form of sexual titillation — as in the farces Ben Travers wrote in the twenties (see *Rookery Nook*). The once very popular Whitehall farces of the fifties and sixties, such as *Simple Spymen* or *Chase Me Comrade*, are again fundamentally 'innocent': characters may repeatedly be manoeuvred into situations which suggest sexual impropriety — they may frequently and literally find themselves caught with their trousers down — but the adulterous liaison which appears so glaringly obvious is nearly always the result of a complex but *falsely* incriminating set of circumstances. In other words, they *look* as though they're being naughty but in fact they're not — they are merely unlucky or unwise. Indeed, unlike *Loot*, these plays draw upon and are largely sustained by accepted notions of conventional morality. The classic form of English farce thrives in a social world which possesses rigid, clearly-defined standards (especially in relation to sexuality) so that, when characters are threatened with a tumble from the tight-rope they tread precariously, the beckoning fall involves not only loss of respectability and scandal, but the break-up of family relationships.

Farce meets black comedy

In *Loot*, Orton introduced into this garden of innocence a
forbidden fruit derived from the theatre of the absurd and from
black comedy. Absurdist drama, as it influenced Orton in the work
of playwrights such as Beckett and Jean Genêt, stresses the
alienation of man in a world devoid of meaning. As Eugène
Ionesco, also an important practitioner in this genre, observed in
connection with Kafka: 'Cut off from his religious, metaphysical
and transcendental roots, man is lost; all his actions become
senseless, absurd, useless'. Black comedy often goes hand in hand
with this view of mankind's plight: areas of life normally
sacrosanct or taboo are subjected to humour or cynicism. In *Loot*,
the iconoclastic attitudes towards death and bereavement, piety
and the Roman Catholic church, and towards authority in general
and the police in particular, are clearly intended by Orton to shock
conventional opinion and to encourage a sense of moral anarchy.
Orton enjoyed parading his allergy to sacred cows. He made the
McLeavys Catholics partly because he wanted to chip away at the
claims of the Roman Catholic church to an infallible authority, and
partly because Catholicism, above all other forms of Christianity,
provided him with a rich source of ritual observance and
nomenclature which he could readily satirise and subvert. It is
clearly Orton's view that the sentiments of bereavement commonly
invested in a traditional funeral are largely a hypocritical sham. So
he turns Mrs McLeavy's funeral into the material of farce, pushing
through to a grotesque extreme the Joycean pun of a funeral
becoming 'fun for all', with lots of comic business involving a glass
eye and the corpse's dentures used as castanets.

Orton's bad taste is calculated. He enjoyed seeing 'what he
could get away with' and he delighted in outwitting the censor, a
game in which he revealed considerable creative zest. At the time
Orton was writing, the Lord Chamberlain had to 'pass' all plays
before they could be produced on the public stage: in his 'Author's
Note' (see p.88) Orton sets out the cuts which were required by the
censor, thus demonstrating the ponderously arbitrary and
unintentionally hilarious way in which official morality attempts
to defend itself. Whether Orton's play of the sixties still retains its
power to shock is a question we will return to, but it is clear that
much depends on individual sensibility. Orton's comic treatment of
taboo subjects has provoked the charge from some quarters that
Loot is a heartless and 'sick' play. For others Orton's humour is the
product either of a sniggering schoolboy mentality or of a nasty

mind, intent on trivialising everything. Orton is certainly capable of
arousing extreme responses. Here is Martin Esslin in his essay 'Joe
Orton: The Comedy of (Ill) Manners' speaking for the prosecution:

> [Orton] articulates, in a form of astonishing elegance and
> eloquence, the same rage and helpless resentment which
> manifests itself in the wrecked trains of football supporters, the
> mangled and vandalized telephone kiosks and the obscene
> graffiti on lavatory walls . . . Behind Orton's attack on the
> existing state of humanity in the West there stands nothing but
> the rage of the socially and educationally under-privileged . . .
> Orton exemplifies the spiritual emptiness and — in spite of his
> obvious brilliance and intelligence — the thoughtlessness, the
> inability to reason and to analyse, of these deprived multitudes.

On the other hand, Orton's apologists claim that his humour
contains positive and even purifying elements. John Lahr, in his
introduction to *Entertaining Mr Sloane*, sums up his own response
to Orton's work:

> To him, nothing was sacred; but the fury of his attack, its
> peculiar combination of joy and horror, was not without a
> broader spiritual motive. Orton wanted to shock the society and
> also to purify it. On stage, his characters are performing animals.
> And, once the beast in every man is faced, then tolerance can
> more easily replace righteousness . . . In showing us how we
> destroy ourselves, Orton's plays are themselves a survival tactic.
> He makes us laugh to make us learn. There is salvation in that.

Characterization

A moral perspective
Because plot predominates in farce, character is presented as a
series of broad types in whom it would be a mistake to expect
psychological depth. Characters in farce generally possess an
artificial 'larger than life' quality, involving an exaggeration of one
single element or 'humour' of human nature; yet, while in a
conventional farce we might expect character to be pushed in the
direction of grotesque caricature, we would be very surprised to
find numbered among its *dramatis personae* the following: two
homosexual criminals, one of whom has fathered five illegitimate
children, yet who are both presented as possessing a kind of
cherubic insouciance; a corrupt policeman for whom the bestowing

of casual but violent beatings seems to be all in the line of a normal day's investigation; and a woman who, though nominally a nurse and a Roman Catholic, imitates the action of the praying mantis in her many marital relationships and dispatches her patients speedily, once she has ensured that she is favoured in their wills.

Orton makes farce serve his own purposes, and the farce convention that characters are to be observed 'from the outside' is turned to his own creative advantage in at least two ways. First, Orton's characterisation serves to demonstrate his view that character is not some absolute central essence or unchanging combination of traits; it is rather, in his judgment, the tactical adoption of different rôles in order to serve self-interest. Second, it is through his presentation of character that Orton portrays the nature of the world he believes we inhabit. The characters in *Loot* operate on an automatic circuit: they are motivated by the straightforward workings of their appetites — for money, for sex, for power over others. Only McLeavy adheres superficially to any conventional kind of morality, and Orton is out to discredit him. Right from the opening of the play it is clear that McLeavy's sanctimoniously inflated opinion of his own moral worth is fraudulent. What do his feelings of bereavement, for instance, really amount to? The roses on the wreaths seem to be the principal object of his concern; he obviously begrudges every penny of the expense to which the funeral has put him; and had events worked out differently (as indeed was the case in an earlier draft of the play), he would have been quite prepared to race into a hasty second marriage with Fay. This is not to suggest, however, that McLeavy is a hypocrite: his naivety and stupidity prevent any awareness on his part of the contradictions between his avowed, conformist propriety and the more nakedly unguarded expressions of feeling that, from time to time, escape him. Yet Orton does not want his audience to fail to appreciate his hollowness as a spokesman for a certain kind of received public morality and orthodoxy.

The moral basis on which other characters act is more direct; it is perfectly encapsulated in the terms of Truscott's reply to McLeavy just after Truscott has struck a deal with the criminals to share the loot:

> MCLEAVY: Has no one considered my feelings in all this?
> TRUSCOTT: What percentage do you want? (p.83)

The joke here is that for Truscott there is no joke at all: no other feelings exist for Truscott save those which derive from self-interest. Except for McLeavy, the characters in the play modify their roles and follow remorselessly the line — as they perceive it — dictated by acquisitiveness, lust or the desire to dominate others. Fay, for example, may shift her 'affections', but even though she keeps up appearances when necessary, she freely adopts any manipulative role which will win her maximum advantage. Her 'character', like that of the others in the play, is a purely behaviouristic phenomenon: it is what appears on the surface — no more, no less. And in Truscott's case, his whole character is self-conceived precisely in terms of a performance: his characteristic yet transparent strategem is to pretend to know more than he does; he wishes to act out the part of the masterful sleuth which he believes himself to be. The humour arises as this impossible fantasy falls apart before our very eyes.

Comic deflation

Orton's puppets may articulate stylishly and amusingly, but spontaneous feeling is generally beyond their compass. Although it may at first appear, for instance, that Truscott works up a powerful head of emotion in his bouts of interrogatory assault and battery, the abiding impression is one of routine violence dispensed with the coldness of an automaton. Equally, one feels that both Hal and Dennis are insulated from what most people would regard as a flow of genuine emotion. Dennis may claim, for example, to be suffering from the disappointment of sexual rejection (p.33), but it is all sent up with knowing playfulness. The appropriate mask is worn for a second, and then discarded with a wink or a grimace.

Though increasingly the characters in the play are involved in frenzied action and bizarre complications, their inner life remains an arctic void, a place devoid of all 'natural' humane feeling. In fact, much of the special atmosphere of *Loot* derives from an incongruity between the frantic twitchings on the surface of the play's action and the icy depths beneath; there is a disparity between the pressures of mounting crisis — involving a funeral, a robbery and its detection — and the clinically understated, deadpan or even non-existent responses of the characters, considered from a normal human standpoint. This is an area in which Orton's characteristic comic deflation operates throughout the play; he frequently allows us to glimpse for an ironic moment the expected conventional reaction to a situation, and then in an instant blacks out this response by demonstrating that his characters simply do not respond according to that anticipated set of values. To take one of the more outrageous examples, consider the episode in which Fay, Dennis and Hal are just about to stash the loot in the casket which has previously contained the contents of Mrs McLeavy's stomach (p.79). When Hal wipes the inside of the casket with Dennis's handkerchief, Dennis exclaims: 'Oh, you've gone too far! Using my handkerchief for that.' For a second we may asssume that Dennis is objecting to the gross tastelessness of what Hal has just done and the outrage it offers to Hal's mother's memory; but Dennis continues a second later — 'It was a birthday present'. His objection is, after all, strictly practical and based on a mere concern for *his* property; nobody else's feelings enter into the matter. The characteristic placing by Orton of the stock phrase ('It was a birthday present') in the incongruous context, so that it trails behind it a spurious sentimentality, only adds to the humour. With the careful timing of the well-laid comic device, the expected humane response is exploded in an instant.

McLeavy: the comic butt

Only McLeavy, the comic outsider, responds according to a conventional, expected pattern, but Orton mocks his glib words as they fall from his mouth. Only McLeavy, the comic butt, really experiences overmastering feeling, as for instance when his tolerance of Truscott's overbearing intrusions finally snaps (p.52), or when he faces the dilemma of whether to become an accessory to the crime by lying to cover up his son's guilt (pp.77-8); but on both occasions Orton clearly intends us to find McLeavy's anger or anguish ludicrous, because his response singularly fails to acknowledge the all-pervasively corrupt morality of 'the way of the world'. McLeavy's function as the representative of a residual 'norm' of certain social, religious and moral values is a vital element in *Loot* (and one which Orton's final play, *What the Butler Saw*, lacks, much to its detriment). Farce needs at least one character susceptible to outrage, a quality McLeavy possesses in abundance. Hal remarks wryly on his father's lack of self-control when his conventional expectations are overturned — 'his generation takes a delight in being outraged' (p.74) — and even Truscott on several occasions tries to disabuse McLeavy of his mindlessly complacent acceptance of authority: 'Your son seems to have a more balanced idea of the world we live in than you do, sir.' (p.74) Perhaps earlier in the play Truscott was inclined to take McLeavy's bowing and

scraping at the door of Authority as a mere hypocritical mouthing
of platitudes, but when Truscott realises that McLeavy really
believes these things he says, he becomes in the police inspector's
eyes a kind of dangerous lunatic.

> MCLEAVY: The police are for the protection of ordinary
>   people.
> TRUSCOTT: I don't know where you pick up these slogans,
>   sir. You must read them on hoardings. (p.86)

It is too late for poor McLeavy to unlearn the slogans. Truscott
works on the assumption that everyone knows it is merely a useful
fiction that high standards of morality are maintained in public
life; but nobody has ever told McLeavy about this conspiracy.
Believing as he does in justice, conscience and the natural triumph
of virtue, McLeavy can never make sense of the world in which
Orton makes him move. That is why McLeavy is reduced finally to
believing that he exists in a totally inexplicable universe as the
victim of 'some kind of interplanetary rag'.

The play may glance briefly and sardonically in the direction of
McLeavy's moral orthodoxy — 'Even if they [the bank robbers]
aren't caught, they'll suffer . . . such people never benefit from
their crime' (p.17) — and for an untypical moment even Fay may
suspect that poetic justice rules (p.42), but by the end of Loot
any scheme of that kind is overturned. It is the innocent McLeavy
who is carried off screaming to prison — and probably to a
conveniently arranged death — while the criminals and the corrupt
policeman calmly share out the spoils. Orton gives to his winners
the implicit knowledge that to show even the most superficial,
McLeavy-style allegiance to a received morality is disabling and
that to exhibit the faintest sign of being at the mercy of
spontaneous or humane feeling is to make yourself a victim in a
world governed by appetite.

Self-interest rules

Loot may certainly present us with a satiric distortion of the actual
facts of real life, as we know them, but as we have already seen, the
play is used as a vehicle to communicate a nihilistic moral position.
It might be argued at this point that Orton is attacking the
disorders and brazen self-interest of his society in a salutary way by
making them appear absurd and by showing the extent to which
they violate any acceptable standards of morality. In satiric
comedy this is a familiar tactic — in Ben Jonson's Volpone (1607),

for instance, which though separated from *Loot* by three and a half centuries presents an illuminating contrast with it. In Jonson's play Volpone pretends to be fatally ill so as to elicit gifts from his would-be heirs. He dupes those who attempt to fawn on him, in the process making his victims reveal the corrupt lengths to which they will go in order to satisfy their avarice in a society in which cupidity seems to have reached epidemic proportions. Volpone shows such enterprise, wit and energy that for a time he may almost entirely win over an audience's sympathy; yet finally there is a patterning of moral values in Jonson's play which will lead to Volpone's fall and force a recognition of the monstrous culpability of Volpone's own avarice. For Orton, however, there can be no absolute position from which any binding moral judgment can be made. This is the very basis of Orton's anarchism. So, while *Loot* may certainly be viewed as an attack on those who complacently accept authority — this note is sounded throughout the play — there is finally no argument against anarchic domination by naked self-interest. That, Orton would seem to say with an amused shrug, is the way things are.

A judgment on Truscott?
An awareness of this kind may help us clarify our reaction to Truscott at the end of the play. On the one hand, Orton clearly enjoyed baiting the police. When *Loot* won the *Evening Standard* award as the best play of 1966, Orton recorded in his diary that he made some remarks along these lines at the award ceremony: 'We sent a few [complimentary tickets] to Scotland Yard. And the police loved the play so much that they rang up asking for more tickets. Everyone else thinks the play is a fantasy. Of course, the police know that it's true.' At the end of the play Orton knows — and enjoys the fact — that many members of the audience will be shocked that a policeman should behave as Truscott does and escape scot-free. On the other hand, shock at Truscott's behaviour should be only our first, provisional response. Orton challenges the audience to examine its reaction. What is the basis for our shock? In the world the play has delineated, is not Truscott acting in a totally understandable and acceptable way? In the way, Orton suggests, all survivors really behave — whether they are brazen about it, or shelter behind the facade of 'appearances'? In Truscott's conduct at the end of the play we find no cant, none of the bourgeois moralizing, which the play has discredited, about the rights and wrongs of the case; there is 'straightforwardly' the

striking of a good deal and the grasping of a favourable percentage.
Now there will be some who, like myself, do not share Orton's
nihilistic vision; we may know or hope that the world is different
from the one he portrays. Yet Orton's final manoeuvre is certainly
an interesting challenge. Has he not obliged us, within the terms
which the play lays down, to find Truscott's actions winning our
slightly uncomfortable endorsement?

Language and humour

A tradition of High Comedy

> FAY (*to* MCLEAVY): You see how far things have progressed?
>   Your son won't obey you. (*To* HAL.) Are you still refusing
>   to attend your mother's funeral?
> HAL: Yes.
> FAY: What excuse do you give?
> HAL: It would upset me.
> FAY: That's exactly what a funeral is meant to do.
> MCLEAVY: He prefers to mourn in private.
> FAY: I'm not in favour of private grief. Show your emotions in
>   public or not at all. (p.10)

In this fairly characteristic exchange from early in the play, does
the dialogue strike us as representing the way such characters
would really speak in this situation? Not quite. Behind the dialogue
there are certainly reminders of the ordinary formulations of daily
discourse, but the level of formality is raised a couple of notches;
the language begins to approach an epigrammatic poise which
signals the playwright's pleasure in linguistic manoeuvres. Orton
took painstaking care over the construction and balance of his
dialogue. We have already noted that his early taste in prose was
for the mannered style of a Ronald Firbank; his dramatic
influences are strongly centred in that great tradition of High
Comedy which runs from the Restoration to Wilde's *The
Importance of Being Earnest* (1895). Orton was particularly
attracted to playwrights who possessed their own distinctive style
and a sense of literary panache. A list of such influences would
include William Wycherley (1640-1716) — see *The Country Wife*
(1675) — William Congreve (1670-1729), whose *The Way of the
World* (1700) is perhaps *the* great comedy of manners, Richard
Brinsley Sheridan (1751-1816) — see *The Rivals* (1775) and *The
School for Scandal* (1777) — and, of course, Oscar Wilde
(1854-1900).

Orton quite properly insisted that each dramatist must find his own style and that to a large extent the style is the man: 'The style must ring of the man, and if you think in a certain way and you write true to yourself . . . then you will get a style, a style will come out.' Yet, as many critics have observed, Orton's borrowings from the tradition briefly sketched in above are sometimes very direct. At the lowest level, though perhaps sanctioned by a time-honoured comic licence, Orton has few scruples about what amounts to direct plagiarism, as a comparison of the two following extracts reveals: The first passage occurs in the opening scene of Wycherley's *The Country Wife*; the second is taken from *Loot* (p.82).

SIR JASPER: Pray salute my wife, my lady, sir.
MR HORNER: I will kiss no man's wife, sir . . .
SIR JASPER: . . . Not know my wife, sir?
MR HORNER: I do know your wife, sir; she's a woman, sir . . .

HAL: With such an intelligent wife you need a larger income.
TRUSCOTT: I never said my wife was intelligent.
HAL: Then she's unintelligent? Is that it?
TRUSCOTT: My wife is a woman. Intelligence doesn't really
    enter into the matter.

Sometimes, in a more sophisticated fashion, the echo of an earlier dramatist's lines may improve the jest. In *The Importance of Being Earnest* (Act III), Lady Bracknell defends her nephew Algernon's integrity as follows:

JACK: . . . the fact is that I do not approve at all of his moral
    character. I suspect him of being untruthful.
LADY BRACKNELL: Untruthful! My nephew Algernon?
    Impossible! He is an Oxonian.

— a line Orton wittily recalls in this exchange (*Loot*, p.70):

TRUSCOTT: Stealing public money. And that is just what your
    son and his accomplices have done.
MCLEAVY: Harold would never do a thing like that. He
    belongs to the Sons of Divine Providence.

Those who know Wilde's masterpiece well will discover in *Loot* just how deeply Orton had absorbed *The Importance of Being Earnest*. Consider the two following extracts:

LADY BRACKNELL (*pencil and notebook in hand*): I feel

bound to tell you that you are not down on my list of
eligible young men, although I have the same list as the dear
Duchess of Bolton has. We work together, in fact. However, I
am quite ready to enter your name, should your answers be
what a really affectionate mother requires. Do you smoke?

JACK: Well, yes, I must admit I smoke.

LADY BRACKNELL: I am glad to hear it. A man should
always have an occupation of some kind. There are far too
many idle men in London as it is. How old are you?

JACK: Twenty-nine

LADY BRACKNELL: A very good age to be married at. I have
always been of the opinion that a man who desires to get
married should know either everything or nothing. Which do
you know?

JACK (*after some hesitation*): I know nothing, Lady Bracknell.

LADY BRACKNELL: I am very pleased to hear it. I do not
approve of anything that tampers with natural ignorance.
Ignorance is like a delicate exotic fruit; touch it and the
bloom is gone. (*Earnest*, Act I)

FAY: You've confirmed my worst fears. You have no job. No
prospects. And now you're about to elope to the Continent
with a casual acquaintance and not even a baby as
justification. Where will you end? Not respected by the
world at large like your father. Most people of any influence
will ignore you. You'll be forced to associate with young
men like yourself. Does that prospect please you?

HAL: I'm not sure.

FAY: Well, hesitation is something to be going on with. We can
build on that. What will you do when you're old?

HAL: I shall die.

FAY: I see you're determined to run the gamut of all
experience. That can bring you nothing but unhappiness.
You've had every chance to lead a decent life and rejected
them. I've no further interest in your career. (*Loot*, p.12)

Both passages depend heavily for their humour on the way in
which clichés of the given situation are made to lie down side by
side with something more epigrammatic — an epigram being a
balanced, pithily formulated statement in which an idea is neatly
encapsulated. And what Orton has learnt from Wilde is the effect
that can be produced by making the epigram the vehicle for a kind
of inspired inanity. Both Lady Bracknell and Fay seem perfectly

sure of the ground on which they stand, but the humour is
produced by a subtle mockery of the inquisitorial tone both ladies
adopt and by a sending up of the stock assumptions which lie
behind, in the one case, an assessment of a young man's eligibility,
and in the other, a condemnation of decadent living.
Sententiousness is pushed towards absurdity; its pontifications are
neatly punctured. The use of paradox is one of the main methods
by which this particular effect is achieved — and paradox functions
by leading us into seemingly absurd or apparently self-contradictory
statements. So, in both examples quoted above we will find certain
expectations set up in the first part of a statement or in a question,
which are quickly followed by a reversal of those expectations or
by an incongruous twist — for instance, the notion that smoking
may be commended as an 'occupation' or that death represents
running 'the gamut of all experience'.

The tang of the Ortonesque

High comedy derives much of its effect from an interplay of
urbane, well-turned repartee between characters on stage. Look
carefully at this short section of dialogue which occurs just before
the passage previously quoted from *Loot* (p.12).

> FAY: Have you known him long?
> HAL: We shared the same cradle.
> FAY: Was that economy or malpractice?
> HAL: We were too young then to practise, and economics still
>   defeat us.

This exchange which culminates in Hal's capping retort, with its sly
insinuation about the precociously early formation of his
homosexual relationship with Dennis, shows a most precise
rhythmic balancing in its question and response format. The
underlying joke behind much of Orton's dialogue is that characters
are frequently made to speak with a wit and style which seems
above their station — and sometimes beyond their understanding.
The devices of high comedy are often combined in *Loot* with an
earthier, more colloquial language than we would expect to meet
with in any true comedy of manners, but whether characters
deliver their frequently outrageous sentiments with polished *élan*
or with vulgar garrulousness, there is behind the words only an
emotional and moral void. Orton likes to create an amusing
incongruity between elements of stylisation in his dialogue and the
outlandish or morally squalid subject matter it transmits. We need

also to be alive to the quick juxtapositions of different levels of
language which so often create the special tang of the 'Ortonesque'.

To give some life to these generalisations, consider, for instance,
the scene in which Fay is undressing the corpse of Mrs McLeavy
behind the screen while Hal, chatting away libidinously about his
fantasies of owning his ideal brothel, receives the various articles of
clothing.

> HAL: I'd have two Irish birds. A decent Catholic. And a
> Protestant. I'd make the Protestant take Catholics. And the
> Catholic take Protestants. Teach them how the other half
> lives. I'd have a blonde bird who'd dyed her hair dark. And a
> dark bird who'd dyed her hair blonde. I'd have a midget. And
> a tall bird with big tits.
>
> > FAY *hands across the screen in quick succession, a pair of
> > corsets, a brassiere and a pair of knickers.* HAL *puts them
> > into the pile.*
>
> FAY: Are you committed to having her teeth removed?
> HAL: Yes.
>
> > *Pause*
>
> I'd have a French bird, a Dutch bird, a Belgian bird, an
> Italian bird —
>
> > FAY *hands a pair of false teeth across the screen.*
>
> — and a bird that spoke fluent Spanish and performed the
> dances of her native country to perfection. (*He clicks the
> teeth like castanets.*) I'd call it the Consummatum Est. (p.39)

The main ingredient of the comedy here is, of course, the blackness
of the humour: it derives from the characters' cold-blooded
reduction of the corpse to the level of a mere object deprived of all
its former human connections. The comic frisson is intensified,
however, by the intrusion into Hal's slangy, staccato chatter of
Fay's 'Are you committed to having her teeth removed?' The more
appropriate, matching register for Fay to adopt here would
probably lead her to say something like: 'Do you really want me to
take the teeth out?'; but Orton's style of humour rejoices in
precisely that jarring note produced by the echo of prissy
officialese in the phrasing of Fay's question. Notice too how Hal's
speech here, before its blasphemous final reference, takes a quick
turn into something like the mode of a travel brochure — '. . .

performed the dances of her native country to perfection'.

Characters in the play may seem to be extremely self-conscious about language. Orton frequently makes them embark on the longer speeches they are given — Fay's confession would be a good example (p.67) — with a kind of operatic relish which openly proclaims the theatricality of the world of artifice through which they move. They sometimes even comment on the language used by others: for instance, Truscott applauds Fay's confession of guilt in a manner which seems to mark her style out of ten (while also making an ironic comment on the whole play): 'Very good. Your style is simple and direct. It's a theme which less skilfully handled could've given offence' (p.67). Earlier Fay herself had instructed McLeavy, as he began his proposal: 'Use any form of proposal you like. Try to avoid abstract nouns' (p.31). Yet this kind of linguistic expertise does not generally extend to any awareness on the characters' part of how their *own* language will affect listeners — in this case, most particularly, the audience. The essence of the humour in Fay's question to Hal about the teeth resides precisely in her own obvious obliviousness to the oddity of the idiom she uses.

The battle of words
In his diary Orton clearly delighted in jotting down snippets of conversation, culled from the talk of his neighbours or overheard on the bus. His sensitive antennae liked to pick up remarks which signalled the thinness of their speakers' lives. He particularly enjoyed detecting how unintended elements of stiltedness, pomposity or grotesqueness can intrude into the banality of everyday discourse. Sometimes in *Loot* we will feel that Orton is sharing with us a careful re-assemblage of some of his prize snatches; he will often surround them with contrasting formal and stylized elements of language; yet he invites us to become eavesdroppers on characters who irresistibly are given to speak in a telling variety of ways, but who are not given to knowing what their speech tells us about them. McLeavy's speech, for instance, is simply a rehashing in cliché of the assumptions of a certain kind of received popular 'wisdom', though Orton allows even this discredited supporter of authority to spark into something like epigrammatic life — significantly when McLeavy briefly begins to question the *status quo* (p.60). Yet normally McLeavy's verbal vapidity is a gauge of Orton's disapproval. Other characters score points off him easily in the skirmishes of repartee that run through

the play. Truscott, for example, who in these battles of wit can be
nimbly adroit or ponderously obtuse, according to the comic
demands of a situation — there is something neurotically unhinged
and unpredictable about this man who is both psychopath and
clown — invariably gets the better of McLeavy (see, for instance,
the exchange quoted on page xxiii).

The quick-fire repartee which is such a feature of the play can
consist of the snappy riposte — a kind of service-volley technique —
or of rallies of more extended duration. In the case of the longer
set-piece of dialogue, one device that Orton puts to frequent use in
Loot is the sort of argument which gathers impetus through a
series of rapid exchanges, often in short pithy sentences, yet while
it proceeds according to a pseudo-logic, ends either circularly or in
an absurd conclusion. Dialogue of this kind is often aimed at
showing the sophistry with which authority, in the form of
Truscott, defends its position. Such exchanges repeatedly possess
an 'Alice in Wonderland' flavour, one of the most effective being
the *non sequitur* which leads to Dennis 'proving' to Truscott that
the police inspector is a 'responsible person' (pp.52-3).

Some comic weaponry
The visual nature of much of the humour in *Loot* should not be
underestimated. As well as the involved comic business centring
around attempts to hide the loot or the corpse (or both
simultaneously), there are many smaller but telling touches of
visual humour, some of which border on slapstick. Nonetheless, the
most memorable comedy in the play is undoubtedly verbal, and
accurate timing and delivery of the lines are of paramount
importance if a production of the play is to be a success. Orton
deploys nearly all the weaponry in the comic writer's armoury. The
play is studded with the paradoxical epigrams that Orton learnt
from Wilde how to polish — 'Had euthanasia not been against my
religion I would have practised it. Instead I decided to murder
her' (p.67). Besides the comic devices we have already examined,
Orton also shows how successfully humour may be extracted
from the old technique of having characters talking at cross-
purposes (p.56); he is a master of the *double-entendre* ('I'm a great
believer in traditional positions' — p.31); he can press into service
the groan-producing pun ('Whose mummy is this?' — p.43) or the
grotesque comic simile ('Most people would at least flinch upon
seeing their mother's eyes and teeth handed around like nuts at
Christmas' — p.84); and he delights in the new-minting of cliché

which gives an everyday or journalistic phrase a new life
('Complete extinction has done nothing to silence her slanderous
tongue' – p.64). This last point is an important one, for as well as
having an ear well-tuned to those excesses of cliché in speech which
could, when transposed a little, sound a grotesque comic note,
Orton was always alive to the possibilities of giving a new slant to a
formula from the popular press, an advertising slogan or a piece of
hackneyed dialogue from a Hollywood film. Many of the most
quotable lines from *Loot* have behind them the ring of the well-
known phrase or saying – for instance, 'God is a gentleman. He
prefers blondes' (p.70) or 'She's practised her own form of
genocide for a decade and called it nursing' (p.66). On occasions
parody is writ large in the play, as when Truscott is made to
introduce himself with a send-up of Sherlock Holmes (p.26), but
pastiche may work in more subtle ways. Orton possessed a magpie
facility for bringing together all sorts of different elements in his
dialogue: within the space of a few lines a recall of the elegant wit
of Wilde may rub shoulders with a spoof of the cornier kind of
exchange from an old 'second feature' film. Seen in this light, *Loot*
often appears to resemble a patchwork of sophisticated travesties.

Critical differences

Towards a consensus?
During its provincial tour in 1966, *Loot* was born to a controversial
reception. After the play's appearance in Bournemouth, a headline
in *The Times* thundered 'BOURNEMOUTH OLD LADIES
SHOCKED', above an article which told of the premature exit
from the Pavilion Theatre of some two dozen members of the
audience who were outraged by 'dialogue which uses the word
brothel and which satirizes sex, patriotism, death and the law'.
Orton grew wearily accustomed to this kind of response – if the
play had been going well he probably would have enjoyed it – and
John Lahr records that Orton used to call this regularly protesting
part of his audience 'The Bump and Trot Brigade', a reference to
the noise their seats made as angry spectators left the theatre.
When the play nearly expired completely at Wimbledon in March,
1966, the London *Evening News* delivered what was obviously
intended to be the death-blow: 'Personally I thought it was one of
the most revolting things I had ever seen . . . The management
pasted over the bills at Wimbledon: "This show is unsuitable for
children" . . . It would have been better if Michael Codron had

displayed some new ones: "THIS PLAY IS UNSUITABLE".'
(Michael Codron was the producer of this first, ill-fated *Loot*.) A
different production of the play which opened later that year in
London won considerable acclaim (see page ix), and there were a
number of reviewers who were prepared to recognize *Loot*'s
qualities. Alan Brien, writing in the *Sunday Telegraph* found the
play to be 'the most genuinely quick-witted, pungent and sprightly
entertainment by a new young British playwright for a decade';
while Ronald Bryden in the *Observer* gave Orton a tag which was
to stick: this dramatist was the 'Oscar Wilde of Welfare State
gentility'.

A revival of *Loot* in the spring of 1984 at the Ambassadors
Theatre, with Leonard Rossiter starring in the role of Truscott,
provided an opportunity of assessing whether, almost two decades
after the play was written, any kind of critical consensus had
emerged. In fact, though the production was almost universally
praised, the nature of the play itself still obviously aroused a
diverse range of responses.

For Irving Wardle, writing in a review for *The Times*, *Loot*'s
power to shock 'is as strong as ever . . . the comedy derives from a
deadly serious warning on the hazards of placing a blind trust in
authority . . . The boldness of the plotting remains amazing' and
for Robert Hewison 'there is a hard political centre to *Loot*'
which achieves a 'subversive effect' (*Sunday Times*). Giles Gordon
wrote in the *Spectator* that 'it's as accomplished and sociologically
exact a play as any written since the second world war'. Other
critics were not so favourably impressed. Michael Billington, in
his *Guardian* review, felt that 'although Orton tilts subversively at
death, the Church, the British police and the whole judicial system,
his gibes gradually acquire a mechanical heartlessness'. In the
Observer, Victoria Radin was convinced the play had dated: '*Loot*
is a stylishly but aridly written period-piece which startled the
smug Sixties, but which looks smug itself in the disorder of the
Eighties. It needs to be given a long rest'. This was a view stated in
more muted terms by Rosalind Carne in the *New Statesman*: 'it
felt dated . . . for all its brilliance of invention and structure,
Loot's element of shock has receded'.

Orton brought to heel?
The charges of 'mechanical heartlessness' and aridity have been
brought against *Loot* ever since its first appearance, and it will not
surprise us that a play which sets out to administer shock

treatment should record readings which depend on the sensibility of the individual critic. However, it was not shock that Sheridan Morley felt; in his review in *Punch* Morley clearly believed that *Loot* could now be safely tucked up in bed for the night: it was really 'just another missing-body romp', a play firmly 'in the traditions of British farce . . . The play is in fact a lot closer to Ben Travers than was appreciated in the shock-horror of its original and scandalized reception eighteen years ago . . . [Orton] was essentially a cobbler of unusually stylish Whitehall farces, and in that context the other claims that have been made for him in the years since his appalling murder are beginning to look a little exaggerated'.

No doubt the kind of 'claims' that Morley refers to here are those made for Orton by such critics as John Lahr for whom Orton offers 'salvation' (see page xix). Lahr sometimes too facilely confers on Orton a kind of self-sacrificial, heroic status, writing, for instance, that 'like the votaries of Dionysus, Orton was hounded by his passion. In his plays, Orton faced his rage and exorcised it in his lethal wit'. Claims of this kind are bound to produce a counter-reaction, as with anything promoted as being dangerously and outrageously innovatory — a patronising smile followed by the dismissal that the product is after all very familiar, despite its slightly new packaging. This was, in fact, much the line taken by Martin Esslin in 1966 in a review of *Loot* in *Plays and Players*. Esslin granted that the portrayal of Truscott deeply shocked the audience — though it might be noted that, following certain well-publicised scandals involving police corruption, today's audience may have less faith to lose in the forces of law and order — and yet for Esslin 'Orton's play is harmless, old-fashioned fun, *Arsenic and Old Lace* superficially modernised'.

Both Morley and Esslin are attempting to defuse what Orton clearly hoped would be a lethal dramatic explosion. To shock and even outrage an audience was a rôle Orton foreshadowed for himself as a playwright when, in one of those novels he could never get published,* he makes his protagonist, Gombold, contemplate the far greater firing power words might possess in the theatre than simply on the page:

> . . . Then there was the problem of gathering enough of the
> enemy together in order that they might listen. He started
> wondering where and how he could hit the enemy most . . . He

*The novel was finally published in 1971, under the title of *Head to Toe*.

thought of a book. But that was no use . . . the book might not
be read . . . But if you could lock the enemy into a room somewhere and fire the sentence at them you could get a sort of
seismic disturbance.

The Orton who wrote this would probably have been disturbed by
the bland assertion that he was, after all, simply another Ben
Travers with a sprinkling of black humour added. Possibly Orton
would have felt that this response indicated the subtle power the
English bourgeosie possesses to infiltrate, and finally to occupy
on its own terms, territory which has supposedly been mined by
the enemy within. Certainly, like Sheridan Morley, the *Daily
Telegraph* reviewer, John Barber, experienced no 'seismic
disturbance' after witnessing Jonathan Lynn's 1984 production of
Loot; instead, Barber commented, 'all this [the complex action of
the play] whirls along with the merry insouciance and jingling
pace of a holiday roundabout. Holiday is the key word. We cannot
be shocked by the play's outrageous bad taste because the mood is
all playtime and capricious escape.' No sign of alienation or *angst*
there.

   It is probably idle speculation to wonder exactly how Orton
would have felt about the kind of response to *Loot* which knocks
the play back as mere entertainment that can be consumed with no
anxiety or harmful after-effects. It is likely that the iconoclastic
Orton underestimated the distancing effect of the conventions of
farce. Endless travesty and spoof add further to an audience's
sense that the play creates a highly artificial world in which
characters have an interplanetary remoteness which makes any
sense of identification out of the question. Moreover, *Loot*
deflects, or even destroys, our normal responses, without providing
us with any other framework of judgment except for the law of the
jungle; so that the very members of the audience Orton wishes to
feel threatened will perhaps finally be reduced to feeling — if they
feel anything deeply at all — that the play is simply a 'romp' and
that they have been given a licence to laugh in a light-hearted,
superficial fashion. Perhaps, recognizing this, Orton's anarchic self
might have been driven to deliver still more stinging rabbit punches
in an attempt to make the bourgeois laugh on the other side of his
face. Possbily that was what he tried to do in his final, flawed
farce, *What the Butler Saw*. However, Orton was given to the idea
that character was multi-faceted, and in another of his selves —
that of the calculating playwright who at the time of the original

London production of *Loot* was so preoccupied with the daily
figures for box-office takings — he would perhaps have been
vastly entertained by the terms on which the *Daily Telegraph*
reviewer appreciated *Loot* in 1984, and he might well have found
his own uses for the review — not least through the voice of some
updated Edna Welthorpe. There is, of course, no necessary
contradiction between a desire for both artistic and financial
success; yet Orton's essential approach to life and the theatre
was brazen, exploitative and uncomplying. He wanted to wave two
elegant fingers at the bourgeoisie while they paid him hand over
fist for so doing. Although the *Daily Telegraph* reviewer, perhaps
wilfully, chose to ignore this aspect of *Loot,* there are on the other
wing more earnest votaries who attempt to transform Orton by a
process of hagiography into an icon to be placed in some Dionysian
shrine dedicated to moral anarchism. I think Orton might have
waved two fingers at them too.

Further reading

Orton's own work
Orton: Complete Plays (Methuen, 1976), with a useful introduction by John Lahr contains:-
The Ruffian on the Stair (first pub. 1966, radio version; revised 1967)
Entertaining Mr Sloane (1964)*
The Good and Faithful Servant (1970)
Loot (1967)*
The Erpingham Camp (1967)
Funeral Games (1970)
What the Butler Saw (1969)*

*Also published individually in Methuen's Modern Plays series

Fred & Madge; *The Visitors*, intro. Francesca Coppa (two plays; Nick Hern Books, 1998)
Between Us Girls (stories; Methuen, 2000)
Up Against It (screenplay; Methuen, 1979)
Head to Toe (novel, originally entitled *The Vision of Gombold Proval*; Methuen, 1986)
Joe Orton and Kenneth Halliwell, *The Boy Hairdresser*; *and Lord Cucumber* (two novels; Methuen, 2001)
John Lahr (ed.), *The Orton Diaries* (Methuen, 1986)
John Lahr, *Diary of a Somebody* (based on *The Orton Diaries*; Methuen, 1989)

Writing about Orton's work
John Lahr's biography of Orton, *Prick Up Your Ears* (Allen Lane, 1978; Bloomsbury, 2002) is essential reading.
C.W.E. Bigsby, *Joe Orton* (Methuen, 1982)
Maurice Charney, *Joe Orton* (Macmillan, 1984)
Francesca Coppa (ed.) *Joe Orton: A Casebook* (Routledge, 2003)
Simon Shepherd, *Because We're Queers: The Life and Crimes of Kenneth Halliwell and Joe Orton* (GMP Publishers, 1989)

The following four books are recommended because they contain commentaries on Orton's work together with other material which should help to fill in the background to the drama of the period:

C.W.E. Bigsby (ed.), *Contemporary English Drama* (Arnold, 1981) contains an essay by Martin Esslin, 'Joe Orton: The Comedy of (Ill) Manners'

Benedict Nightingale, *A Reader's Guide to Fifty Modern British Plays* (Heinemann Educational, 1982; first published by Pan Books as *An Introduction to Fifty Modern British Plays* in the Pan Literature Guides series)

John Russell Taylor, *The Second Wave* (Methuen, 1971)

Katherine Worth, *Revolutions in Modern English Drama* (G. Bell, 1973)

Video

Loot (screenplay by Ray Galton and Alan Simpson, dir. Silvio Narizzano, starring Richard Attenborough, Lee Remick, Hywel Bennett and Milo O'Shea; Warner Home Video, 1989, 97 mins, colour)

Above: Dennis screws down the coffin lid (p.21). *Right:* Hal kneels at the coffin (p.23).

Above: Fay and McLeavy (p.31). *Right:* Hal clicks the false teeth like castanets (p.39). *Below:* Hal, Fay and the corpse (p.39).

Left: Fay supports the heavily bandaged McLeavy (p.48).
Above: Truscott takes McLeavy's statement (p.49).

Left: Truscott examines the glass eye (p.58). *Above:* Hal kneels to McLeavy (p.75). *Below:* Truscott discovers the loot (p.81).

Above: McLeavy berates Truscott (p.83). *Below:* McLeavy is arrested (p.85).

Loot

To Peggy

Act One

A room in MCLEAVY'S *house. Afternoon.*

Door left with glass panel. Door right. A coffin stands on trestles. MCLEAVY, *in mourning, sits beside an electric fan.*

FAY, *in a nurse's uniform, enters from the left.*

FAY. Wake up. Stop dreaming. The cars will be here soon. (*She sits.*) I've bought you a flower.

MCLEAVY. That's a nice thought. (*Taking the flower from her.*)

FAY. I'm a nice person. One in a million.

She removes her slippers, puts on a pair of shoes.

MCLEAVY. Are those Mrs McLeavy's slippers?

FAY. Yes. She wouldn't mind my having them.

MCLEAVY. Is the fur genuine?

FAY. It's fluff, not fur.

MCLEAVY. It looks like fur.

FAY. (*standing to her feet*). No. It's a form of fluff. They manufacture it in Leeds.

She picks up the slippers and takes them to the wardrobe. She tries to open the wardrobe. It is locked. She puts the slippers down.

You realize, of course, that the death of a patient terminates my contract?

MCLEAVY. Yes.

FAY. When do you wish me to leave?

MCLEAVY. Stay for a few hours. I've grown used to your company.

FAY. Impossible. I'm needed at other sickbeds. Complain to the Society if you disagree with the rules.

She picks up his coat, holds it out for him to put on.

You've been a widower for three days. Have you considered a second marriage yet?

MCLEAVY (*struggling into his coat*). No.

FAY. Why not?

MCLEAVY. I've been so busy with the funeral.

FAY. You must find someone to take Mrs McLeavy's place. She wasn't perfect.

MCLEAVY. A second wife would be a physical impossibility.

FAY. I'll hear none of that. My last husband at sixty came through with flying colours. Three days after our wedding he was performing extraordinary feats.

She takes the coathanger to the wardrobe. She tries to open the wardrobe door, frowns, puts the coathanger beside her slippers.

You must marry a girl with youth and vitality. Someone with a consistent attitude towards religion. That's most important. With her dying breath Mrs McLeavy cast doubt upon the authenticity of the Gospels. What kind of wife is that for you? The leading Catholic layman within a radius of forty miles. Where did you meet such a woman?

MCLEAVY. At an informal get-together run by a Benedictine monk.

FAY takes the flower from his hand and pins it on to his coat.

FAY. Was she posing as a Catholic?

MCLEAVY. Yes.

FAY. She had a deceitful nature. That much is clear. We mustn't let it happen again. I'll sort out some well-meaning young woman. Bring her here. Introduce you. I can visualize her – medium height, slim, fair hair. A regular visitor to some place of worship. And an ex-member of the League of Mary.

MCLEAVY. Someone like yourself?

FAY. Exactly. (*She takes a clothes brush and brushes him down.*) Realize your potential. Marry at once.

MCLEAVY. St Kilda's would be in uproar.

FAY. The Fraternity of the Little Sisters is on my side. Mother Agnes-Mary feels you're a challenge. She's treating it as a specifically Catholic problem.

MCLEAVY. She treats washing her feet as a Catholic problem.

FAY. She has every right to do so.

MCLEAVY. Don't Protestants have feet then?

FAY. The Holy Father hasn't given a ruling on the subject and so, as far as I'm concerned, they haven't. Really, I sometimes wonder whether living with that woman hasn't made a free thinker of you. You must marry again after a decent interval of mourning.

MCLEAVY. What's a decent interval?

FAY. A fortnight would be long enough to indicate your grief. We must keep abreast of the times.

She takes the brush to the wardrobe and tries to open it.

(*Turning, with a frown.*) Who has the key to this cupboard?

MCLEAVY. Harold.

FAY. Why is it locked?

MCLEAVY. He refused to give a reason.

MCLEAVY *shakes the wardrobe door.*

FAY. Your son is a thorn in my flesh. The contents of his dressing-table are in indictment of his way of life. Not only firearms, but family-planning equipment. A Papal dispensation is needed to dust his room.

She goes out left. MCLEAVY *follows her. She can be heard calling:*

(*Off.*) Harold! (*Farther off.*) Harold!

> HAL *enters right. He goes to the wardrobe, unlocks it, looks in, and locks the wardrobe again. He stands beside the coffin and crosses himself.* FAY *and* MCLEAVY *re-enter left.*

FAY (*pause, with a smile*). Why is the wardrobe locked?

HAL. I've personal property in there.

MCLEAVY. Open the door. There's enough mystery in the universe without adding to it.

HAL. I can't. You wouldn't wish to see. It's a present for your anniversary.

MCLEAVY. What anniversary?

HAL. Your being made a knight of the Order of St Gregory.

MCLEAVY. I'm not convinced. Open the wardrobe.

HAL. No.

FAY (*to* MCLEAVY). You see how far things have progressed? Your son won't obey you. (*To* HAL.) Are you still refusing to attend your mother's funeral?

HAL. Yes.

FAY. What excuse do you give?

HAL. It would upset me.

FAY. That's exactly what a funeral is meant to do.

MCLEAVY. He prefers to mourn in private.

FAY. I'm not in favour of private grief. Show your emotions in public or not at all.

HAL (*to* MCLEAVY). Another wreath has arrived.

MCLEAVY. Is it roses?

HAL. Roses and fern.

MCLEAVY. I must look.

> *He goes out left.*

FAY. I sometimes think your father has a sentimental attachment to roses.

HAL. Do you know what his only comment was on my mother's death?

FAY. Something suitable, I'm sure.

She takes the mattress cover from the mattress and folds it.

HAL. He said he was glad she'd died at the right season for roses. He's been up half the night cataloguing the varieties on the crosses. You should've seen him when that harp arrived. Sniffing the petals, checking, arguing with the man who brought it. They almost came to blows over the pronunciation.

FAY hangs the folded mattress cover over the screen.

If she'd played her cards right, my mother could've cited the Rose Growers' Annual as co-respondent.

FAY. The Vatican would never grant an annulment. Not unless he'd produced a hybrid.

HAL (*at the coffin, looking in*). Why was she embalmed?

FAY. She asked to be scientifically preserved after her last attack.

HAL stares into the coffin, deep in thought. FAY joins him.

You couldn't wish her life. She was in agony since Easter.

HAL. Yes, the egg I presented to her went untouched.

FAY. On doctor's orders, I can tell you in confidence.

Pause.

Sit down, Harold. I want a word with you. Your father can't be expected to help at the moment.

HAL sits. FAY sits opposite him.

(*Folding her hands in her lap.*) The priest at St Kilda's has asked me to speak to you. He's very worried. He says you spend your time thieving from slot machines and deflowering the daughters of better men than yourself. Is this a fact?

HAL. Yes.

FAY. And even the sex you were born into isn't safe from your
marauding. Father Mac is popular for the remission of sins,
as you know. But clearing up after you is a full-time job. He
simply cannot be in the confessional twenty-four hours a day.
That's reasonable, isn't it? You do see his point?

HAL. Yes.

FAY. What are you going to do about this dreadful state of
affairs?

HAL. I'm going abroad.

FAY. That will please the Fathers. Who are you going with?

HAL. A mate of mine. Dennis. A very luxurious type of lad.
At present employed by an undertaker. And doing well in
the profession.

FAY. Have you known him long?

HAL. We shared the same cradle.

FAY. Was that economy or malpractice?

HAL. We were too young then to practise, and economics still
defeat us.

FAY. You've confirmed my worst fears. You have no job. No
prospects. And now you're about to elope to the Continent
with a casual acquaintance and not even a baby as justification. Where will you end? Not respected by the world at
large like your father. Most people of any influence will
ignore you. You'll be forced to associate with young men like
yourself. Does that prospect please you?

HAL. I'm not sure.

FAY. Well, hesitation is something to be going on with. We
can build on that. What will you do when you're old?

HAL. I shall die.

FAY. I see you're determined to run the gamut of all experience.
That can bring you nothing but unhappiness. You've had
every chance to lead a decent life and rejected them. I've no
further interest in your career. (*She rises to her feet.*) Call
your father. He's surely had enough of the company of
plants for the present.

HAL goes to the door left.

HAL (*calling*). Eh, Dad!
FAY. Shhh! This is a house of mourning.

HAL returns and sits.

The priest that came to pay his condolences had such quiet tones that at first I thought they'd sent along a mute.

MCLEAVY enters carrying a large wreath marked off into numbered squares.

MCLEAVY. The Friends of Bingo have sent a wreath. The blooms are breathtaking.

He puts the wreath down. Sits. Takes out a newspaper. FAY, *standing beside the coffin, looking into it, silently moves her lips in prayer, a rosary between her fingers.*

(*With a loud exclamation.*) Another catastrophe has hit the district! Bank robbers have got away with a fortune.
FAY (*looking up*). Which bank?
MCLEAVY. Next door to the undertakers. They burrowed through. Filled over twenty coffins with rubble.
FAY. Rubble?
MCLEAVY. From the wall. Demolished the wall, they did.
FAY. People are so unbalanced these days. The man sitting next to you on the bus could be insane.
MCLEAVY. Where the money has gone is still occupying the police. It's one of the big gangs, I expect.
HAL. What do you known of the big gangs? It's a small gang. Minute.
FAY. Do you know the men concerned?
HAL. If I had that money, I wouldn't be here. I'd go away.
FAY. You're going away.
HAL. I'd go away quicker.
FAY. Where would you go?

HAL. Spain. The playground of international crime.

FAY. Where are you going?

HAL. Portugal.

Pause.

You'll have to get up early in the morning to catch me.

Door chimes. HAL *goes to the window, draws back the curtains and looks out.*

Dennis is here with the cars.

FAY. Is he driving?

HAL. Yes. He looks impressive. Close proximity to death obviously agrees with him.

He goes out left.

MCLEAVY (*putting away the newspaper*). What's the plan for the afternoon?

FAY. The funeral will occupy you for an hour or so. Afterwards a stroll to the house of a man of God, a few words of wisdom and a glance through the Catholic Truth Society's most recent publication should set your adrenalin flowing. Then a rest. I don't want you overstrained.

MCLEAVY. When did you say you were leaving? I don't wish to cause you any inconvenience.

FAY. I'll decide when you've inconvenienced me long enough.

MCLEAVY. You're very good to me.

FAY. As long as you appreciate my desire to help. My own life has been unhappy. I want yours to be different.

MCLEAVY. You've had an unhappy life?

FAY. Yes. My husbands died. I've had seven altogether. One a year on average since I was sixteen. I'm extravagant you see. And then I lived under stress near Penzance for some time. I've had trouble with institutions. Lack of funds. A court case with my hairdresser. I've been reduced to asking people for money before now.

MCLEAVY. Did they give it to you?

FAY. Not willingly. They had to be persuaded. (*With a bright smile.*) I shall accompany you to your lawyers. After the reading of your wife's will you may need skilled medical assistance.

MCLEAVY (*with a laugh*). I don't think there are any surprises in store. After a few minor bequests the bulk of Mrs McLeavy's fortune comes to me.

FAY. I've also arranged for your doctor to be at your side. You've a weak heart.

>   DENNIS *enters left.*

DENNIS. Good afternoon. I don't want to be too formal on this sad occasion, but would you like to view the deceased for the last time?

>   FAY *takes out a handkerchief.*
>   HAL *enters.*

(*To* HAL.) Give us a hand into the car with the floral tributes.

>   HAL *takes out several wreaths,* DENNIS *picks up the rest.*

(*To* FAY.) We'll need help with the coffin. (*Nods to* MC-LEAVY.) He's too near the grave himself to do much lifting.

FAY. Harold can carry his mother to the car.

DENNIS. A charming suggestion. (*To* MCLEAVY.) If you'll be making your last good-byes while I give them a hand?

>   *Takes the wreaths to the door.* HAL *enters left.*

(*Passing* HAL *in the doorway.*) I want a word with you.

>   DENNIS *goes out left.* HAL *is about to follow him.*

FAY (*calling*). Come and see your mother, Harold. You'll never see her again.

MCLEAVY, HAL *and* FAY *stand beside the coffin, looking in.*

She looks a treat in her W.V.S uniform. Though I'd not
care to spend Eternity in it myself.

HAL. She's minus her vital organs, isn't she?

FAY. It's a necessary part of the process.

MCLEAVY. Where are they?

FAY. In the little casket in the hall. Such tranquillity she has.
Looks as though she might speak.

MCLEAVY (*taking out a handkerchief, dabbing his nose*). God
rest the poor soul. I shall miss her.

FAY. Death can be very tragic for those who are left.

They bow their heads in silence.

HAL. Here, her eyes are blue. Mum's eyes were brown. That's
a bit silly, isn't it?

FAY. I expect they ran out of materials.

MCLEAVY. Are her eyes not natural, then?

FAY. No. (*With a smile, to* HAL.) He's such an innocent, isn't
he? Not familiar with the ways of the world.

MCLEAVY. I thought they were her own. That surprises me.
Not her own eyes.

DENNIS *enters with a screwdriver.*

DENNIS. The large harp we've placed on top of the motor. On
the coffin we thought just the spray of heather from her
homeland.

MCLEAVY. It's going to take me a long time to believe she's
dead. She was such an active sort of person.

FAY (*to* DENNIS). You're going abroad, I hear?

DENNIS. Yes.

FAY. Where did you get the money?

DENNIS. My life insurance has matured.

MCLEAVY (*to* DENNIS). Tragic news about your premises. Was
the damage extensive?

DENNIS. The repair bill will be steep. We're insured, of course.

MCLEAVY. Was your Chapel of Rest defiled?

DENNIS. No.

MCLEAVY. Human remains weren't outraged?

DENNIS. No.

MCLEAVY. Thank God for that. There are some things which deter even criminals.

DENNIS. I'm concerned with the actual furnishings damaged – I mean, the inside of the average casket is a work of art – time and labour, oh, it makes you weep.

MCLEAVY. The bodies laid out. Waiting for burial. It's terrible thoughts that come to me.

DENNIS. It broke my heart. Dust and rubble.

MCLEAVY. What a terrible thing to contemplate. The young men, thinking only of the money, burrowing from the undertakers to the bank. The smell of corruption and the instruments of death behind them, the riches before them. They'd do anything for money. They'd risk damnation in this world and the next for it. And me, a good man by any lights, moving among such people. They'll have it on their conscience. Even if they aren't caught, they'll suffer.

DENNIS. How?

MCLEAVY. I don't know. But such people never benefit from their crimes. It's people like myself who have the easy time. Asleep at nights. Despite appearances to the contrary, criminals are poor sleepers.

FAY. How do you sleep, Harold?

HAL. Alone.

DENNIS. We'll be leaving in a short time, Mr McLeavy. I'd like to satisfy myself that everything is as it should be. We pride ourselves on the service.

MCLEAVY. What clothes would they wear, d'you suppose? Dust is easily identified. They'd surely not work in the nude? God have mercy on them if they did. Even to avoid the hangman I'd not put up with precautions of that nature.

FAY. They'd wear old clothes. Burn them after.

MCLEAVY. If you could get a glance between their toes you'd find the evidence. But to order a man to remove his clothes isn't within the power of the police. More's the pity, I say. I'd like to see them given wider powers. They're hamstrung by red tape. They're a fine body of men. Doing their job under impossible conditions.

HAL. The police are a lot of idle buffoons, Dad. As you well know.

MCLEAVY. If you ever possess their kindness, courtesy and devotion to duty, I'll lift my hat to you.

DENNIS. I'm going to batten down the hatches now.

MCLEAVY (*glancing into the coffin*). Treat her gently. She was very precious to me.

He goes out left.

FAY (*following* MCLEAVY, *turning in the doorway*). I'll be consoling your father if I'm needed. Be careful what you talk about in front of the dead.

She goes out left.
DENNIS opens a packet of chewing-gum, puts a piece in his mouth, takes off his hat.

DENNIS. Lock the door.

HAL. It won't lock.

DENNIS. Put a chair under the handle. We're in trouble

HAL wedges a chair under the handle.

We've had the law round our house.

HAL. When?

DENNIS. This morning. Knocked us up they did. Turning over every bleeding thing.

HAL. Was my name mentioned?

DENNIS. They asked me who my associate was. I swore blind

I never knew what they were on about. 'Course, it's only a matter of time before they're round here.

HAL. How long?

DENNIS. Might be on their way now. (*He begins to screw down the lid of the coffin.*) Don't want a last squint, do you? No? Where's the money?

HAL taps the wardrobe.

In there? All of it? We've got to get it away. I'll lose faith in us if we get nicked again. What was it last time?

HAL. Ladies' overcoats.

DENNIS. See? Painful. Oh, painful. We were a laughing-stock in criminal circles. Banned from that club with the spade dancer.

HAL. Don't go on, baby. I remember the humiliating circumstances of failure.

DENNIS. We wouldn't have been nicked if you'd kept your mouth shut. Making us look ridiculous by telling the truth. Why can't you lie like a normal man?

HAL. I can't, baby. It's against my nature.

He stares at the coffin as DENNIS screws the lid down.

Has anybody ever hidden money in a coffin?

DENNIS looks up. Pause.

DENNIS. Not when it was in use.

HAL. Why not?

DENNIS. It's never crossed anybody's mind.

HAL. It's crossed mine.

He takes the screwdriver from DENNIS, and begins to unscrew the coffin lid.

It's the comics I read. Sure of it.

DENNIS (*wiping his forehead with the back of his hand*). Think of your mum. Your lovely old mum. She gave you birth.

HAL. I should thank anybody for that?

DENNIS. Cared for you. Washed your nappies. You'd be some kind of monster.

> HAL *takes the lid off the coffin.*

HAL. Think what's at stake.

> *He goes to wardrobe and unlocks it.*

Money.

> *He brings out the money.* DENNIS *picks up a bundle of notes, looks into the coffin.*

DENNIS. Won't she rot it? The body juices? I can't believe it's possible.

HAL. She's embalmed. Good for centuries.

> DENNIS *puts a bundle of notes into the coffin. Pause. He looks at* HAL.

DENNIS. There's no room.

> HAL *lifts the corpse's arm.*

HAL (*pause, frowns*). Remove the corpse. Plenty of room then.

DENNIS. Seems a shame really. The embalmers have done a lovely job.

> *They lift the coffin from the trestles.*

There's no name for this, is there?

HAL. We're creating a precedent. Into the cupboard. Come on.

> *They tip the coffin on end and shake the corpse into the wardrobe. They put the coffin on the floor, lock the wardrobe and begin to pack the money into the coffin.*

DENNIS. What will we do with the body?

HAL. Bury it. In a mineshaft. Out in the country. Or in the marshes. Weigh the corpse with rock.

DENNIS. We'll have to get rid of that uniform.

HAL (*pause*). Take her clothes off?

DENNIS. In order to avoid detection should her remains be discovered.

HAL. Bury her naked? My own mum?

He goes to the mirror and combs his hair.

It's a Freudian nightmare.

DENNIS (*putting lid upon coffin*). I won't disagree.

HAL. Aren't we committing some kind of unforgivable sin?

DENNIS. Only if you're a Catholic.

HAL (*turning from the mirror*). I am a Catholic. (*Putting his comb away.*) I can't undress her. She's a relative. I can go to Hell for it.

DENNIS. I'll undress her then. I don't believe in Hell.

He begins to screw down the coffin lid.

HAL. That's typical of your upbringing, baby. Every luxury was lavished on you – atheism, breast-feeding, circumcision. I had to make my own way.

DENNIS. We'll do it after the funeral. Your dad'll be with the priest.

HAL. O.K. And afterwards we'll go to a smashing brothel I've just discovered. Run by a woman who was connected with the Royal Family one time. Very ugly bird. Part Polish. Her eyes look that way. Nice line in crumpet she has. (*He sits astride the coffin.*)

DENNIS. I can't go to a brothel.

HAL. Why not?

DENNIS. I'm on the wagon. I'm trying to get up sufficient head of steam to marry.

HAL. Have you anyone in mind?

DENNIS. Your mum's nurse.

HAL. She's older than you.

DENNIS. An experienced woman is the finest thing that can happen to a lad. My dad swears by them.

HAL. She's three parts Papal nuncio. She'd only do it at set times.

DENNIS. Oh, no. She does it at any time. A typical member of the medical profession she is.

HAL. You've had her ? (DENNIS *grins*.) Knocked it off ? Really ?

DENNIS. Under that picture of the Sacred Heart. You've seen it ?

HAL. In her room. Often.

DENNIS. On Wednesday nights while you're training at St Edmund's gymnasium.

They lift the coffin back on to the trestles.

I'd like to get married. It's the one thing I haven't tried.

HAL. I don't like your living for kicks, baby. Put these neurotic ideas out of your mind and concentrate on the problems of everyday life. We must get the corpse buried before tonight. Be in a tricky position else. And another stretch will be death to my ambitions. I put my not getting on in life down to them persistently sending me to Borstal. I might go permanently bent if this falls through. It's not a pleasant prospect, is it ?

The coffin is back upon the trestles.
DENNIS *takes the chewing-gum from his mouth and sticks it under the coffin. He puts on his hat.* HAL *sits.*

Was it Truscott searched your house ?

DENNIS. Yes. And he had me down the station for questioning. Gave me a rabbit punch. No, I'm a liar. A rabbit-type punch. Winded me. Took me by the cobblers. Oh, 'strewth, it made me bad.

HAL. Yes, he has a nice line in corporal punishment. Last time he was here he kicked my old lady's cat and he smiled while he did it. How did he get into your house ?

DENNIS. He said he was from the sanitary people. My dad let him in. 'Course, I recognized him at once.

HAL. Did you tell him?

DENNIS. Yes.

HAL. What did he say?

DENNIS. Nothing. He kept on about testing the water supply. I asked him if he had a warrant. He said the water board didn't issue warrants.

HAL. You should've phoned the police. Asked for protection.

DENNIS. I did.

HAL. What did they say?

DENNIS. They said that one of their men called Truscott was at our house and why didn't we complain to him?

HAL. What did Truscott say?

DENNIS. He said he was from the water board. My nerves were in shreds by the end of it.

> FAY *approaches the door left. Her shadow is cast on the glass panel.*

FAY (*off*). What are you doing, Harold?

> HAL *goes to the coffin and kneels in prayer.*

HAL. That brothel I mentioned has swing doors. (*He bows his head.*) You don't often see that, do you?

> DENNIS *takes the chair from under the door handle and opens the door quietly.*

DENNIS. We're ready now.

> FAY *enters in mourning with a veil over her hair. She carries an embroidered text. Her dress is unzipped at the back. She goes to the wardrobe and tries to open the door. She sees in the mirror that her dress is unzipped, comes to the coffin and bows her head over it.* HAL, *still kneeling, zips her dress up.* MCLEAVY *enters blowing his nose, a sorrowful expression upon his face.*

MCLEAVY (*to* DENNIS). Forgive me being so overwrought, but it's my first bereavement.

DENNIS. The exit of a loved one is always a painful experience.

FAY, *the dress zipped, straightens up.*

FAY. Here – (*she puts the embroidered text on to the coffin.*) – the Ten Commandments. She was a great believer in some of them.

HAL *and* DENNIS *lift the coffin.*

MCLEAVY (*greatly moved, placing a hand on the coffin*). Goodbye, old girl. You've had a lot of suffering. I shall miss you.

HAL *and* DENNIS *go out with the coffin.* FAY *throws back her veil.*

FAY. She's gone. I could feel her presence leaving us. Funny how you know, isn't it?

MCLEAVY. That dress is attractive. Suits you. Black.

FAY. It's another piece of your late wife's finery. Some people would censure me for wearing it. (*She puts a hand on his arm, smiles.*) Are you feeling calmer now?

MCLEAVY. Yes. I've a resilient nature, but death upsets me. I'd rather witness a birth than a death any day. Though the risks involved are greater.

TRUSCOTT *enters left.*

TRUSCOTT. Good afternoon.

FAY. Good afternoon. Who are you?

TRUSCOTT. I am attached to the metropolitan water board. I'm on a fact-finding tour of the area. I'd like to inspect your mains supply.

MCLEAVY. It's outside.

TRUSCOTT. Is it?

Pause, ruminates.

I wonder how it came to be put out there. Most ingenious. You're sure there isn't a tap in this cupboard?

He tries the wardrobe door and smiles.

MCLEAVY. It's in the garden.

TRUSCOTT. Where?

MCLEAVY. I don't know.

TRUSCOTT. I suggest, then, that you find it, sir. Any property belonging to the council must be available on demand. The law is clear on that point.

MCLEAVY. I'll find it at once, sir. I wouldn't wish to place myself outside the law.

He goes off right.

TRUSCOTT (*turning to* FAY). Who has the key to this cupboard?

FAY. The son of the house.

TRUSCOTT. Would he be willing to open it? I'd make it worth his while.

FAY. I've already asked for it to be opened. He refused point-blank.

TRUSCOTT. I see. (*Chews his lip.*) Most significant. You'll be out of the house for some considerable time this afternoon?

FAY. Yes. I'm attending the funeral of my late employer.

TRUSCOTT. Thank you, miss. You've been a great help. (*He smiles, goes to window.*) Who sent the large wreath that has been chosen to decorate the motor?

FAY. The licensee of the King of Denmark. I don't think a publican's tribute should be given pride of place.

TRUSCOTT. You wouldn't, miss. You had a strict upbringing.

FAY. How do you know?

TRUSCOTT. You have a crucifix.

FAY'S *hand goes to the crucifix on her breast.*

It has a dent to one side and engraved on the back the

words: 'St Mary's Convent. Gentiles Only.' It's not difficult
to guess at your background from such tell-tale clues.

FAY. You're quite correct. It was a prize for good conduct. The
dent was an accident.

TRUSCOTT. Your first husband damaged it.

FAY. During a quarrel.

TRUSCOTT. At the end of which you shot him.

FAY (*taken aback*). You must have access to private information.

TRUSCOTT. Not at all. Guesswork mostly. I won't bore you
with the details. The incident happened at the Hermitage
Private Hotel. Right?

FAY (*a little alarmed*). This is uncanny.

TRUSCOTT. My methods of deduction can be learned by anyone with a keen eye and a quick brain. When I shook your
hand I felt a roughness on one of your wedding rings. A
roughness I associate with powder burns and salt. The two
together spell a gun and sea air. When found on a wedding
ring only one solution is possible.

FAY. How did you know it happened at the Hermitage Private
Hotel?

TRUSCOTT. That particular hotel is notorious for tragedies of
this kind. I took a chance which paid off.

He takes out his pipe and chews on it.

Has it never occurred to you to wonder why all your husbands met with violent deaths?

FAY. They didn't!

TRUSCOTT. Your first was shot. Your second collapsed whilst
celebrating the anniversary of the Battle of Mons. Your
third fell from a moving vehicle. Your fourth took an overdose on the eve of his retirement from Sadler's Wells. Your
fifth and sixth husbands disappeared. Presumed dead. Your
last partner suffered a seizure three nights after marrying
you. From what cause?

FAY (*coldly*). I refuse to discuss my private life with you.

TRUSCOTT. For ten years death has been persistently associated with your name.

FAY. You could say the same of an even moderately successful undertaker.

TRUSCOTT. Undertakers have to mix with the dead. It's their duty. You have not that excuse. Seven husbands in less than a decade. There's something seriously wrong with your approach to marriage. I find it frightening that, undeterred by past experience, you're contemplating an eighth engagement.

FAY. How do you know?

TRUSCOTT. You wear another woman's dress as though you were born to it.

FAY (*wide-eyed with wonder*). You amaze me. This dress did belong to Mrs McLeavy.

TRUSCOTT. Elementary detection. The zip is of a type worn by elderly women.

FAY. You should be a detective.

TRUSCOTT. I'm often mistaken for one. Most embarrassing. My wife is frequently pestered by people who are under the impression that she is a policeman's wife. She upbraids me for getting her into such scrapes. (*He laughs.*) You recognize the daily bread of married life, I'm sure. (*He chews on his pipe for a moment.*) When do you intend to propose to Mr McLeavy?

FAY. At once. Delay would be fatal.

TRUSCOTT. Anything taken in combination with yourself usually results in death.

FAY. How dare you speak to me like this! Who are you?

TRUSCOTT *takes out his notebook and pencil.*

TRUSCOTT (*pleasantly*). I'm a council employee who has let his imagination wander. Please forgive me if I've upset you.

He tears a page from the notebook and hands it to FAY.

Sign this chit.

FAY (*looking at it*). It's blank.

TRUSCOTT. That's quite in order. I want you to help me blindly
without asking questions.

FAY. I can't sign a blank sheet of paper. Someone might forge
my name on a cheque.

TRUSCOTT. Sign my name, then.

FAY. I don't know your name.

TRUSCOTT. Good gracious, what a suspicious mind you have.
Sign yourself Queen Victoria. No one would tamper with
her account.

   FAY *signs the paper and gives it back to* TRUSCOTT.

I think that's all I want from you, miss.

FAY. Will you do one thing for me?

TRUSCOTT. What?

FAY. Let me see you without your hat.

TRUSCOTT (*alarmed*). No. I couldn't possibly. I never take my
hat off in front of a lady. It would be discourteous.

   MCLEAVY *enters right.*

Have you been successful in your search, sir?

MCLEAVY. Yes. Next to my greenhouse you'll find an iron
plaque. Under it is a tap.

TRUSCOTT. Thank you, sir. I shall mention your co-operation
in my next report. (*He touches his hat.*) Good afternoon.

   He goes off right.

MCLEAVY. I hope he finds what he's looking for. I like to be of
assistance to authority.

FAY. We must watch that he doesn't abuse his trust. He showed
no credentials.

MCLEAVY. Oh, we can rely on public servants to behave themselves. We must give this man every opportunity to do his duty. As a good citizen I ignore the stories which bring officialdom into disrepute.

HAL *enters left.*

HAL. There's a delay in starting the car. A flat tyre. (*Taking off his coat.*) We're changing the wheel.

MCLEAVY. I hardly think it proper for a mourner to mend the puncture. Is your mother safe?

HAL. Dennis is guarding the coffin.

MCLEAVY. Be as quick as you can. Your mother hated to miss an appointment.

HAL. The contents of that coffin are very precious to me. I'm determined to see they get to the graveyard without mishap.

He goes off left.

MCLEAVY (*with a smile, shaking his head*). It's unusual for him to show affection. I'm touched by it.

FAY. Mrs McLeavy was a good mother. She has a right to respect.

MCLEAVY. Yes. I've ordered four hundred rose trees to help keep her memory green. On a site, only a stone's throw from the church, I intend to found the 'Mrs Mary McLeavy Memorial Rose Garden'. It will put Paradise to shame.

FAY. Have you ever seen Paradise?

MCLEAVY. Only in photographs.

FAY. Who took them?

MCLEAVY. Father Jellicoe. He's a widely travelled man.

FAY. You mustn't run yourself into debt.

MCLEAVY. Oh, Mrs McLeavy will pay for the memorial herself. The will is as good as proven.

FAY *sits beside him, takes his hand.*

FAY. I don't know whether you can be trusted with a secret, but it would be wrong of me to keep you in the dark a moment longer. Your wife changed her will shortly before she died. She left all her money to me.

MCLEAVY. What! (*Almost fainting.*) Is it legal?

FAY. Perfectly.

MCLEAVY. She must've been drunk. What about me and the boy?

FAY. I'm surprised at you taking this attitude. Have you no sense of decency?

MCLEAVY. Oh, it's God's judgement on me for marrying a Protestant. How much has she left you?

FAY. Nineteen thousand pounds including her bonds and her jewels.

MCLEAVY. Her jewels as well?

FAY. Except her diamond ring. It's too large and unfashionable for a woman to wear. She's left that to Harold.

MCLEAVY. Employing you has cost me a fortune. You must be the most expensive nurse in history.

FAY. You don't imagine that I want the money for myself, do you.

MCLEAVY. Yes.

FAY. That's unworthy of you. I'm most embarrassed by Mrs McLeavy's generosity.

MCLEAVY. You'll destroy the will?

FAY. I wish I could.

MCLEAVY. Why can't you?

FAY. It's a legal document. I could be sued.

MCLEAVY. By whom?

FAY. The beneficiary.

MCLEAVY. That's you. You'd never sue yourself.

FAY. I might. If I was pushed too far. We must find some way of conveying the money into your bank account.

MCLEAVY. Couldn't you just give it to me?

FAY. Think of the scandal.

MCLEAVY. What do you suggest then?

FAY. We must have a joint bank account.

MCLEAVY. Wouldn't that cause an even bigger scandal?

FAY. Not if we were married.

MCLEAVY. Married? But then you'd have my money as well as Mrs McLeavy's.

FAY. That is one way of looking at it.

MCLEAVY. No. I'm too old. My health wouldn't stand up to a young wife.

FAY. I'm a qualified nurse.

MCLEAVY. You'd have to give up your career.

FAY. I'd do it for you.

MCLEAVY. I can give you nothing in return.

FAY. I ask for nothing. I'm a woman. Only half the human race can say that without fear of contradiction. (*She kisses him.*) Go ahead. Ask me to marry you. I've no intention of refusing. On your knees. I'm a great believer in traditional positions.

MCLEAVY. The pains in my legs.

FAY. Exercise is good for them. (MCLEAVY *kneels.*) Use any form of proposal you like. Try to avoid abstract nouns.

HAL *enters left.*

HAL. We're ready. The leader of the Mother's Union has given the signal for tears. (*He picks up his coat.*) We must ride the tide of emotion while it lasts.

FAY. They'll have to wait. Your father is about to propose to me. I think you may stay.

MCLEAVY (*struggling to his feet*). I'm giving no exhibition. Not in front of my son.

HAL. I'm surprised he should wish to marry again. He couldn't do justice to his last wife.

Car horn. DENNIS *enters left.*

DENNIS. Would everybody like to get into the car? We'll have the priest effing and blinding if we're late.

MCLEAVY (*to* FAY). This is so undignified. My wife isn't in her grave.

FAY. And she never will be if you insist on prolonging the proceedings beyond their natural length.

MCLEAVY. I'll propose to you on the way to the cemetery, Nurse McMahon. Will that satisfy you?

DENNIS (*to* FAY). You can't marry him. You know the way I feel about you.

FAY. I couldn't marry you. You're not a Catholic.

DENNIS. You could convert me.

FAY. I'm not prepared to be both wife and missionary.

HAL (*putting an arm round* DENNIS). He's richer than my dad, you know.

FAY. Has he his bank statement on him?

DENNIS. I came out without it.

Car horn.

MCLEAVY. Mrs McLeavy is keeping her Maker waiting. I'll pay my addresses to you after the interment.

Prolonged car horn.

Come on! We'll have a damaged motor horn to pay for next!

FAY. I've decided not to attend. I shall wave. Show my respects from afar.

MCLEAVY. The number of people staying away from the poor woman's funeral is heartbreaking. And I hired a de luxe model car because they're roomier. I could've saved myself the expense.

He goes off left.

DENNIS (*to* FAY). I'd slave for you.

FAY (*pulling on her gloves*). I can't marry boys.

HAL. He'd grow a moustache.

FAY. It really doesn't concern me what he grows. Grow two
if it pleases him.

HAL. Would it please you? That's the point.

FAY. The income from fairgrounds might interest me. Other-
wise a man with two has no more fascination than a man with
one.

DENNIS. A fully productive life isn't possible with a man of
Mr McLeavy's age.

FAY. We shall prove you wrong. He'll start a second family
under my guidance.

HAL. You're wasting your time. He couldn't propagate a row
of tomatoes.

   Car horn.

FAY (*to* DENNIS). Get in the car! I've no intention of marrying
you.

DENNIS (*to* HAL, *in tears*). She's turned me down. She's
broken my heart.

HAL. She doesn't know what she's missing, baby.

DENNIS. But she does! That's what's so humiliating. (*He
wipes his eyes with the back of his hand.*) Well, the funeral is
off as far as I'm concerned.

HAL. You're driving the car. People will notice your absence.

   FAY *is at the wardrobe.*

FAY (*pause*). Where did you get your money?

DENNIS. My auntie left it to me.

FAY. Is that true, Harold?

HAL (*after an inner struggle*). No.

DENNIS. I mean my uncle.

FAY (*to* HAL). Is that true?

HAL (*desperate, looking at* DENNIS). No.

DENNIS. You make our life together impossible. Lie, can't
you?

HAL. I can't, baby. It's my upbringing.

Car horn.

DENNIS. Try to control yourself. If I come back and find you've been telling the truth all afternoon – we're through!

He goes off left. FAY *takes two black-edged handkerchiefs from her handbag, shakes them out, gives one to* HAL.

FAY. Blow your nose. People expect it.

She lowers her veil. They both go to the window. They wave. Sound of a car receding. Pause. FAY *turns from the window. She goes to the wardrobe. She throws off her veil.*

Come here. Open this cupboard.

HAL *puts his handkerchief into his pocket.*

Don't hesitate to obey me. Open this cupboard.

HAL. Why are you so interested?

FAY. I've a coatee in there.

HAL. Really?

FAY. I bought it three days ago. I must change. Mourning gets so grubby if you hang around in it for long.

She looks at HAL *in silence.*

I've got a key. I could see in. Quite easy.

HAL. I've got something in there.

FAY. What?

HAL. A corpse.

FAY. You've added murder to the list of insults heaped upon your family?

HAL. One doesn't have to murder to acquire a corpse.

FAY. You're running a private mortuary, then?

Pause.

Where are you concealing the money?

HAL. In my mother's coffin.
FAY. That'd be an unusual hiding-place.

Pause.

Where is it now ? Answer at once. I shan't repeat my question.
HAL. The money is putting on incorruption. The flesh is still
   waiting.
FAY. Where is it waiting ?
HAL. In that cupboard.
FAY. Open it.
HAL. You have a key.
FAY. I haven't.
HAL. You were lying ?
FAY. Yes.

> HAL *gives her the key. She opens the wardrobe, looks in,*
> *closes the door and screams.*

This is unforgivable. I shall speak to your father.

Pause.

She's standing on her head.
HAL. I concealed nothing from you.
FAY. Your explanation had the ring of truth. Naturally I dis-
   believed every word.
HAL. I want her buried. Are you prepared to help me ?
FAY. Oh, no! I couldn't. This is a case for the authorities.
HAL. You'll never make it to the altar without my help.
FAY. I need no help from you to get a man to bed.
HAL. My father holds it as a cherished belief that a whore is
   no fit companion for a man.
FAY. As a creed it has more to offer than most.
HAL. My mate Dennis has done you. He speaks of it with relish.
FAY. Young men pepper their conversation with tales of rape.
   It creates a good impression.

HAL. You never had the blessing of a rape. I was with him at his only ravishment. A bird called Pauline Ching. Broke a tooth in the struggle, she did. It was legal with you. While Jesus pointed to his Sacred Heart, you pointed to yours.

FAY. I never point. It's rude.

HAL. If I tell my father, he'll never marry you.

FAY. I haven't decided whether I wish to marry your father. Your friend is a more interesting proposition.

HAL. He won't be if you grass to the police.

FAY (*pause*). Blackmail? So early in the game.

> HAL *takes out a comb and goes to the mirror. He combs his hair.*

HAL. I want the body stripped. All I ask is an hour or two of Burke and Hare. It isn't a thing someone of the opposite sex can do. And I'm a relative, which complicates the issue.

FAY. You intend a country burial?

HAL. Yes.

FAY. Suppose a dog were to discover her? When they were out hunting for foxes. Do you set no store by the average foxhound?

HAL. Perfectly preserved body of a woman. No sign of foul play. The uniform we'll burn. The underwear you can keep.

FAY. Your mother's underclothes?

HAL. All good stuff.

FAY. I couldn't. Our sizes vary.

HAL. For the bonfire then. Her teeth can go in the river.

FAY. We're nowhere near the river.

HAL. We can borrow your car.

FAY. Provided you pay for the petrol.

HAL. Right.

FAY. Where will she be?

HAL. In the back seat. (*He puts the comb away.*) She always was a back-seat driver.

He opens the wardrobe and wheels the bed to the wardrobe door.

FAY. What about payment?

HAL. Twenty per cent.

FAY. Thirty-three and a third.

HAL. You can keep her wedding ring.

FAY. Is it valuable?

HAL. Very.

FAY. I'll add it to my collection. I already have seven by right of conquest.

HAL *pulls the screen round the bed.*

Thirty-three and a third and the wedding ring.

HAL. Twenty per cent, the wedding ring and I pay for the petrol?

FAY. Thirty-three and a third, the wedding ring and you pay for the petrol.

HAL. You drive a hard bargain.

FAY. I never bargain.

HAL. Done.

He throws the mattress cover to her.

Put her in that.

FAY *goes behind the screen.*

FAY. I need help to get her out of the cupboard.

HAL *goes behind the screen.*

I'm not taking the head end.

HAL. She won't bite. You have your gloves on.

They lift the corpse from the wardrobe and lay it on the bed. Something drops from it and rolls away.

FAY. What's that?

HAL (*appearing from behind the screen, searching*). Nothing, nothing.

FAY (*poking her head over the screen*). A screw from the coffin, perhaps?

HAL. Was it the wedding ring?

FAY (*looking*). No. Nothing important.

HAL. I'm inclined to agree.

> FAY *goes behind the screen.* HAL *takes a sheet from off the screen and spreads it on the floor.*

FAY (*from behind the screen*). Lovely-shaped feet your mother had. For a woman of her age.

> *She hands a pair of shoes across the screen.* HAL *places them in the centre of the sheet.*

What will you do with the money?

> *She hands a pair of stockings over the screen.*

HAL. I'd like to run a brothel. (*He pushes the stockings into the shoes.*) I'd run a two-star brothel. And if I prospered I'd graduate to a three-star brothel. I'd advertise 'By Appointment'. Like jam.

> FAY *hands a* W.V.S. *uniform across the screen.* HAL *folds it up and puts it into the sheet.*

I'd have a spade bird. I don't agree with the colour bar. And a Finnish bird. I'd make them kip together. To bring out the contrast.

> FAY *hands a slip across the screen.* HAL *puts it into the pile.*

I'd have two Irish birds. A decent Catholic. And a Protestant. I'd make the Protestant take Catholics. And the Catholic take Protestants. Teach them how the other half lives. I'd have a blonde bird who'd dyed her hair dark. And a dark bird who'd dyed her hair blonde. I'd have a midget. And a tall bird with big tits.

FAY *hands across the screen in quick succession, a pair of corsets, a brassiere and a pair of knickers.* HAL *puts them into the pile.*

FAY. Are you committed to having her teeth removed?
HAL. Yes.

Pause.

I'd have a French bird, a Dutch bird, a Belgian bird, an Italian bird—

FAY *hands a pair of false teeth across the screen.*

—and a bird that spoke fluent Spanish and performed the dances of her native country to perfection. (*He clicks the teeth like castanets.*) I'd call it the Consummatum Est. And it'd be the most famous house of ill-fame in the whole of England.

FAY *appears from behind the screen.* HAL *holds up the teeth.*

These are good teeth. Are they the National Health?
FAY. No. She bought them out of her winnings. She had some good evenings at the table last year.

FAY *folds up the screen. The corpse is lying on the bed, wrapped in the mattress cover, tied with bandages.*

HAL (*approaching the bed, bowing his head*). She was a great lady. Nothing was too good for her. Which is why she had to go.
FAY (*taking a key from her handbag, gives it to* HAL). Fetch the car. Pay cash. It's not to be charged to my account.

TRUSCOTT *approaches the door left. His shadow is cast upon the glass panel. He knocks on the door.* HAL *picks up the sheet with the clothes in it. He looks for somewhere to put them.* FAY *opens the door.* TRUSCOTT *stands outside, smiling.*

TRUSCOTT (*touching his hat*). I'm back again, miss.

> FAY *slams the door.* HAL *stuffs the sheet and clothes into the bedpan attached to the invalid chair.* FAY *pulls the screen round the bed.*

(*Calling.*) Might I have a word with you.

> HAL *closes the lid of the bedpan, concealing the clothes.*

FAY (*calling, answering* TRUSCOTT). Yes.

TRUSCOTT. Let me in, then, I can't hold a conversation through a keyhole. I'm a council employee. I might lose my pension.

> HAL *sits in the invalid chair.* FAY *opens the door.* TRUSCOTT *enters.*

What's going on in this house?

HAL. Nothing.

TRUSCOTT. You admit it? You must be very sure of yourself. Why aren't you both at the funeral? I thought you were mourners.

FAY. We decided not to go. We were afraid we might break down.

TRUSCOTT. That's a selfish attitude to take. The dead can't bury themselves, you know.

> *He takes his pipe from his pocket and plugs it with tobacco.*

FAY. What are you doing here?

TRUSCOTT (*smiling*). I've been having a look round your charming house. Poking and prying.

HAL. Have you a search warrant?

TRUSCOTT. What for?

HAL. To search the house.

TRUSCOTT. But I've already searched the house. I don't want to do it again.

FAY. It's common knowledge what police procedure is. They must have a search warrant.

TRUSCOTT. I'm sure the police must, but as I've already informed you, I am from the water board. And our procedure is different.

He puts the pipe into his mouth, lights it, draws on it.

(*Chewing on his pipe.*) Now, I was sent on a fool's errand a few minutes ago. Unless I'm much mistaken, the object of my search is in that cupboard.

Pause.

Open it for me.

HAL. It isn't locked.

TRUSCOTT. I can't take your word for it, lad.

> HAL *opens the wardrobe door.* TRUSCOTT *puts on a pair of spectacles, and stares in. He shakes his head. He takes off his spectacles.*

This puts an entirely different complexion on the matter.

FAY. It's empty.

TRUSCOTT. Exactly. There's still a lot of routine work to be done, I can see that. Would you mind waiting outside, miss? I'd like a word with this lad alone. I'll let you know when you're wanted.

> FAY *and* HAL *exchange bewildered glances.* FAY *goes off left.*

(*Laughing pleasantly.*) I always have difficulties with the ladies. They can't accept a *fait accompli*.

> *Pause. He takes the pipe from his mouth and stares speculatively at* HAL.

What do you know of a lad called Dennis?

HAL. He's a mate of mine.

TRUSCOTT. You don't want to spend your time with a youth like him. He's not your type. He's got five pregnancies to his credit.

HAL. Anyone can make a mistake.

TRUSCOTT. Maybe. But he's obviously getting into the habit of making mistakes. Where does he engender these unwanted children? There are no open spaces. The police patrol regularly. It should be next to impossible to commit the smallest act of indecency, let alone beget a child. Where does he do it?

HAL. On crowded dance floors during the rhumba.

FAY *enters left.*

TRUSCOTT (*removing his pipe, patiently*). I'm a busy man, miss. Do as you're told and wait outside.

FAY. What's your name?

TRUSCOTT. I prefer to remain anonymous for the present.

FAY. Your Christian name.

TRUSCOTT. I'm not a practising Christian.

FAY. Is it Jim?

TRUSCOTT. No.

FAY. A man at the door says it is.

TRUSCOTT. I'd like to help him, but I'm not prepared to admit to any name other than my own.

FAY. He says his name is Meadows.

TRUSCOTT (*pause, nods his head sagely*). One of my names is Jim. Clearly this fellow is in possession of the fact and wishes to air his knowledge. I shall speak to him.

TRUSCOTT *goes off left.*

FAY (*closing the door, whispers*). There's a uniformed policeman at the door! They're on to us.

HAL. It's bluff.

FAY. No. God works for them. They have Him in their pockets like we've always been taught.

HAL. We've got to get rid of him. He'll find the body next.

He opens the wardrobe door and puts FAY'S *shoes and the coathanger inside. He closes the door quickly and turns to* FAY.

Remember when we were wrapping her up?

FAY. It's not something I care to reminisce about.

HAL. Something dropped out? We couldn't find it?

FAY. Yes.

HAL. I know what it was.

FAY. What?

HAL. One of her eyes!

They drop to their knees. They search. TRUSCOTT *enters. They stand.*

TRUSCOTT (*smiling*). Just a bobby making a nuisance of himself.

He goes to the screen and glances behind it. Pause. He takes the pipe from his mouth.

The theft of a Pharaoh is something which hadn't crossed my mind.

He folds the screen revealing the corpse, swathed in the mattress cover and tied with bandages.

Whose mummy is this?

HAL. Mine.

TRUSCOTT. Whose was it before?

HAL. I'm an only child.

TRUSCOTT. A word of warning. Don't take the mickey. You'll make me angry. (*He smiles.*) O.K.?

FAY. It's not a mummy. It's a dummy. I used to sew my dresses on it.

TRUSCOTT. What sex is it?

FAY. I call it 'she' because of my sewing. The garments were female and because I'm literal-minded I chose to believe I was making them on a lady.

TRUSCOTT. Splendid. Excellently put.

HAL. No actual evidence of sex can be given. It's contrary to English law.

TRUSCOTT. Yes, a tailor's dummy provided with evidence of sex would fill the mind of the average magistrate with misgiving. Why is it wrapped?

HAL. We were taking it in the car.

FAY. To a carnival. She's part of a display.

TRUSCOTT. What part?

FAY. A sewing-class. Prewar. The difference in technique is to be demonstrated.

TRUSCOTT. Is this dummy a frequent visitor to exhibitions?

FAY. Yes.

TRUSCOTT. When is the object's outing to take place?

FAY. It isn't going now.

TRUSCOTT. The treat has been cancelled?

FAY. Yes.

TRUSCOTT. Why?

HAL. My mate Dennis was to have arranged transport. He let us down.

TRUSCOTT. I can believe that. From all I've heard of your friend I'd say he was quite capable of disappointing a tailor's dummy.

He puts his pipe into the corner of his mouth. He takes out his notebook and makes notes.

You claim this object is awaiting transport to a carnival where it will be used to demonstrate the continuity of British needlework?

FAY. Yes.

TRUSCOTT. Sounds a reasonable explanation. Quite reasonable.

He puts the notebook away and chews on his pipe. He observes HAL narrowly.

What were you doing on Saturday night?

Pause as HAL tries to avoid telling the truth. He stares at FAY in an agony.

HAL (*at last*). I was in bed.

FAY *breathes a sigh of relief.*

TRUSCOTT. Can you confirm that, miss?

FAY. Certainly not.

TRUSCOTT (*to* HAL). What were you doing in bed?

HAL. Sleeping.

TRUSCOTT. Do you seriously expect me to believe that? A man
of your age behaving like a child? What was your mate doing
on Saturday night?

HAL. He was in bed as well.

TRUSCOTT. You'll tell me next he was sleeping.

HAL. I expect he was.

TRUSCOTT (*to* FAY). What a coincidence, miss. Don't you
agree? Two young men who know each other very well,
spend their nights in separate beds. Asleep. It sounds highly
unlikely to me. (*To* HAL.) What is your excuse for knowing
him?

HAL. He's clever. I'm stupid, see.

TRUSCOTT. Why do you make such stupid remarks?

HAL. I'm a stupid person. That's what I'm trying to say.

TRUSCOTT. What proof have I that you're stupid. Give me an
example of your stupidity.

HAL. I can't.

TRUSCOTT. Why not? I don't believe you're stupid at all.

HAL. I am. I had a hand in the bank job.

FAY *draws a sharp breath.* HAL *sits frozen.* TRUSCOTT
takes his pipe from his mouth.

(*With a nervous laugh.*) There, that's stupid, isn't it? Telling
you that.

TRUSCOTT (*also laughing*). You must be stupid if you expect
me to believe you. Why, if you had a hand in the bank job,
you wouldn't tell me.

FAY. Not unless he was stupid.

TRUSCOTT. But he is stupid. He's just admitted it. He must be
the stupidest criminal in England. Unless – (*He regards* HAL
with mounting suspicion.) – unless he's the cleverest. What
was your motive in confessing to the bank job?

HAL. To prove I'm stupid.

TRUSCOTT. But you've proved the opposite.

HAL. Yes.

TRUSCOTT (*baffled, gnawing his lip*). There's more to this than
meets the eye. I'm tempted to believe that you did have a
hand in the bank job. Yes. I shall inform my superior officer.
He will take whatever steps he thinks fit. I may be required
to make an arrest.

FAY. The water board can't arrest people.

TRUSCOTT. They can in certain circumstances.

FAY. What circumstances?

TRUSCOTT. I'm not prepared to reveal the inner secrets of the
water board to a member of the general public. (*To* HAL.)
Where's the money?

HAL (*closing his eyes, taking a deep breath*). It's being buried.

TRUSCOTT. Who's burying it?

HAL. Father Jellicoe, S.J.

TRUSCOTT. Come here! Come here!

HAL *goes over, his hands trembling as they button up his coat.*

I'm going to ask you a question or two. I want sensible
answers. None of your piss-taking. Is that understood? Do I
make myself plain? I'm talking English. Do you understand?

HAL. Yes.

TRUSCOTT. All right then. As long as we know.

A pause, in which he studies HAL.

Now, be sensible. Where's the money?

HAL *looks at his watch.*

HAL. By now I'd say it was half-way up the aisle of the Church of St Barnabas and St Jude.

He half turns away. TRUSCOTT *brings his fist down on the back of* HAL'S *neck.* HAL *cries out in pain and collapses on to the floor rubbing his shoulder.*

FAY (*indignant*). How dare you! He's only a boy.

TRUSCOTT. I'm not impressed by his sex, miss. (*To* HAL.) I asked for the truth.

HAL. I'm telling the truth.

TRUSCOTT. Understand this, lad. You can't get away with cheek. Kids nowadays treat any kind of authority as a challenge. We'll challenge you. If you oppose me in my duty, I'll kick those teeth through the back of your head. Is that clear?

HAL. Yes.

Door chimes.

FAY. Would you excuse me, Inspector?

TRUSCOTT (*wiping his brow*). You're at liberty to answer your own doorbell, miss. That is how we tell whether or not we live in a free country.

FAY *goes off left.*

(*Standing over* HAL.) Where's the money?

HAL. In church.

TRUSCOTT *kicks* HAL *violently.* HAL *cries out in terror and pain.*

TRUSCOTT. Don't lie to me!

HAL. I'm not lying! It's in church!

TRUSCOTT (*shouting, knocking* HAL *to the floor*). Under any other political system I'd have you on the floor in tears!

HAL (*crying*). You've got me on the floor in tears.

TRUSCOTT. Where's the money?

HAL. I've told you. In church. They're quoting St Paul over it.

TRUSCOTT. I don't care if they're quoting the Highway Code over it. One more chance. Where is it?

HAL (*desperate, trying to protect himself*). In church! In church. My dad's watching the last rites of a hundred and four thousand quid!

> TRUSCOTT *jerks* HAL *from the floor, beating and kicking and punching him.* HAL *screams with pain.*

TRUSCOTT. I'll hose you down! I'll chlorinate you!

> HAL *tries to defend himself, his nose is bleeding.*

You'll be laughing on the other side of your bloody face.

> FAY *enters left, supporting* MCLEAVY, *who is heavily bandaged.*

FAY. They've had an accident!

> TRUSCOTT *leaves* HAL, *pulls the bed from the wall and shoves it to* MCLEAVY, *who faints on to it, just missing the corpse.* HAL *drags the corpse from the bed and shoves it behind the screen.*

TRUSCOTT (*to* MCLEAVY). Have you reported the accident?

> MCLEAVY *opens his mouth. He is too overcome by emotion to speak.*

FAY. It's the shock. Taken away his power of speech, it has.

TRUSCOTT. Has this happened before?

FAY. Yes. Six or seven times.

TRUSCOTT. If he's going to make a habit of it he ought to learn a sign language. (*To* MCLEAVY.) Do you understand me, sir?

> MCLEAVY *closes his eyes, shudders.* TRUSCOTT *straightens up.*

I've known people communicate with the dead in half this time.

MCLEAVY (*moaning*). Oh . . . Oh . . .

TRUSCOTT. What has happened, sir?

MCLEAVY. I've had an accident.

TRUSCOTT. I shall have to make a full report.

He takes out his note-book.

MCLEAVY. Are you qualified?

TRUSCOTT. That needn't concern you at present, sir. I shall let you know later. Now give me a full statement.

MCLEAVY passes a hand across his brow and clears his throat.

MCLEAVY. We set off in high spirits. The weather was humid, a heat mist covered the sky. The road to the graveyard lay uphill. It was a sad occasion for me. In spite of this I kept a tight hold on my emotions, refusing to show the extent of my loss. Along the route perfect strangers had the courtesy to raise their hats. We got admiring glances for the flowers and sympathetic nods for me.

Pause.

The dignity of the event was unsurpassed.

He bows his head, everyone waits. TRUSCOTT *taps sharply on the bedrail with his pencil.*

Then, as the solemn procession was half-way up the hill, a lorry, clearly out of control, came hurtling down on top of us. It struck the first car, holding the remains, and killed the undertaker—

HAL. Not Dennis!

MCLEAVY. No. Mr Walter Tracey. The hearse was a wreck within seconds. Meanwhile the second part of the cortège crashed into the smoking wreckage. I was flung to one side, hitting my head on the bodywork of the vehicle. The next thing I knew I was being helped out by passers-by. The road looked like a battlefield. Strewn with the injured and dying. Blood, glass.

He chokes. Pause.

Several fires were started.

HAL. Was the actual fabric of the coffin damaged?

MCLEAVY. No. Your mother is quite safe.

HAL. No dents? No holes?

MCLEAVY. No. People remarked on the extreme durability of the lid. I was about to give the undertaker a recommendation. Then I remembered that he wasn't capable of receiving one.

TRUSCOTT. Surely he understood when he took on the job that he couldn't make capital out of his own death?

FAY. Where is the coffin?

MCLEAVY. Outside.

FAY (*to* TRUSCOTT). Can it be brought in?

TRUSCOTT. By all means. We mustn't keep a lady waiting.

HAL *goes off.* TRUSCOTT *turns to* MCLEAVY.

Why are you bandaged? Is that a result of the accident?

MCLEAVY. Indirectly. My wounds stem from a fear-crazed Afghan hound that was being exercised at the time. I was bitten about the face and hands. In my nervous state I was an easy target.

TRUSCOTT. Did you take the owner's name?

MCLEAVY. No.

TRUSCOTT. It all seems highly irregular. The dog will have to be destroyed.

MCLEAVY. I don't hold it responsible for its actions. It was frightened.

TRUSCOTT. I've been frightened myself on occasions. I've never bitten anyone. These people should learn to control their pets.

MCLEAVY. The woman who owned the dog had fainted.

TRUSCOTT. She sounds an unstable kind of person to me.

> HAL *and* DENNIS *enter with the coffin. It is charred, blackened and smoking.*

FAY. Who'd think she'd be back so soon?

MCLEAVY. She could never make up her mind in life. Death hasn't changed her.

DENNIS. Your wreaths have been blown to buggery, Mr McLeavy. We might manage a repair job on that big harp.

HAL. What are we going to do for the replay?

MCLEAVY. Buy fresh ones, I suppose. Always some new expense.

> *The coffin is set down. The side falls away, revealing the banknotes inside.* DENNIS *stands in front of the coffin, shielding the contents from* TRUSCOTT *and* MCLEAVY. MCLEAVY *holds out a hand and tries to shake* DENNIS'S *hand.*

(*To* TRUSCOTT.) You must congratulate this boy. He rescued the coffin from the blazing car at considerable personal risk.

TRUSCOTT (*dryly*). If he behaves with such consideration to a dead woman, what might we not expect with a live one?

HAL. We need a finishing touch. Know what it is? A holy image. Centre. Between candles.

FAY. I have a Madonna.

HAL. What could be better? Make a gesture. She knew what disappointment was, didn't she? Same as us. A little imagination. What wonders can't it accomplish.

DENNIS. Oh, yes. We've found in the trade that an impression can be created with quite humble materials: a candle, half a yard of velvet and a bunch of anemones and the effect is of a lying in state.

MCLEAVY. My photo of His Holiness would enhance the scene, only it's three Popes out of date.

FAY. Mrs McLeavy won't mind. She wasn't a woman who followed the fashions. Go and get it.

> MCLEAVY *stands, moves to the door.* TRUSCOTT *bars his path.*

TRUSCOTT. I must ask you to remain where you are. No one is to leave without my permission.

MCLEAVY. Why?

TRUSCOTT. When you disobey my orders, sir, you make my job doubly difficult.

MCLEAVY. On what authority do you give orders?

TRUSCOTT. You'd be considerably happier if you allowed me to do my duty without asking questions.

MCLEAVY. Who are you?

TRUSCOTT. I'm an official of the Metropolitan Water Board, sir, as I've already told you.

MCLEAVY. But the water board has no power to keep law-abiding citizens confined to their rooms.

TRUSCOTT. Not if the citizens are law abiding.

MCLEAVY. Whether they're law abiding or not the water board has no power.

TRUSCOTT. I don't propose to argue hypothetical cases with you, sir. Remain where you are till further notice.

MCLEAVY. I shall take legal advice.

TRUSCOTT. That is as may be. I've no power to prevent you.

MCLEAVY. I want to telephone my lawyer.

TRUSCOTT. I can't allow you to do that. It would be contrary to regulations. We've no case against you.

> TRUSCOTT *chews on his pipe.* MCLEAVY *stares in fury.*

FAY. Can't he fetch the Pope's photo?

TRUSCOTT. Only if some responsible person accompanies him.

HAL. You're a responsible person. You could accompany him.

TRUSCOTT. What proof have I that I'm a responsible person?

DENNIS. If you weren't responsible you wouldn't be given the power to behave as you do.

TRUSCOTT *removes his pipe, considers.*

TRUSCOTT. That is perfectly correct. In which case I shall accompany you, sir. Come with me.

TRUSCOTT *and* MCLEAVY *go off left.*

HAL (*closing the door*). We must return the remains to the coffin and the money to the cupboard.

DENNIS. Why?

FAY. Mr McLeavy may ask for the coffin to be opened. Formaldehyde and three morticians have increased his wife's allure.

DENNIS. But a corpse is only attractive to another corpse.

HAL. We can't rely on him having heard that.

DENNIS *begins to unscrew the coffin lid.* FAY *and* HAL *drag the corpse from behind the screen.*

DENNIS (*looking up*). What's that!

FAY. Mrs McLeavy.

DENNIS (*to* HAL). How much have you told her?

HAL. Everything.

DENNIS. We've never involved a woman in anything unsavoury before.

He takes the lid off the coffin. FAY *piles money into his arms.* HAL *does the same.*

(*To* FAY.) Half of this money is mine. Will you marry me?

HAL. We're splitting the money three ways now, baby. You'll have thirty-four thousand.

DENNIS (*to* FAY). Is that enough?

FAY. You've a slight lead on Mr McLeavy at the moment.

She kisses him. DENNIS *trembles and drops the money back into the coffin.*

HAL (*angry*). Hurry up! What's the matter with you?

DENNIS. My hands are trembling. It's excitement at the prospect of becoming engaged.

HAL. You're too easily aroused. That's your trouble.

    MCLEAVY'S *shadow appears on the glass panel.* DENNIS *tips the money into the coffin.*

MCLEAVY (*off*). I'll complain to my M.P. I'll have you reported.

    HAL *shoves the lid on to the coffin.* MCLEAVY *enters.*

He's turned the water off. I've just been trying to use the toilet—

FAY (*standing in front of him, preventing him seeing the corpse*). Oh, please! You don't have to explain.

    HAL *tries to drag the corpse away.* DENNIS *opens the wardrobe.*

MCLEAVY. I don't believe he's anything to do with the water board. I was handcuffed out there. D'you know that? Hand-cuffed.

    He sees the corpse. He gives a shriek of horror.

What in Heaven's name is that!

FAY. It's my appliance.

MCLEAVY. I've never seen it before.

FAY. I kept it in my room. It was personal.

MCLEAVY. What is it doing down here?

FAY. I'm going to do some work. For charity.

MCLEAVY. What kind of work?

FAY. I'm making the vestments for Our Lady's festival. I was commissioned. My altar cloth at Easter brought me to the attention of the Committee.

MCLEAVY. My congratulations. You'll want plenty of room to work. (*To* DENNIS.) Take Nurse McMahon's applicance to my study.

FAY (*anxious, with a smile*). It's most kind of you, Mr McLeavy, but I'd prefer to work down here. Mrs McLeavy's presence will bring me inspiration.

MCLEAVY. Very well, you have my permission to work down here. I look forward to seeing the finished results.

TRUSCOTT *enters.*

TRUSCOTT (*To* MCLEAVY). Do you still want your padre's photograph, sir?

MCLEAVY. Yes.

TRUSCOTT. You'll find a policeman outside. He will accompany you. Off you go.

MCLEAVY. I resent your manner of speaking! I'm the householder. I can't be ordered about like this.

TRUSCOTT (*shoving him to the door*). Don't make my job any more tiring than it is, sir. Fetch the photograph in question and wait outside until I call.

MCLEAVY *goes off left.*

(*To* DENNIS.) I want a word with you. (*To* HAL *and* FAY.) The rest of you outside!

HAL. Can't I stay with him? He's the nervous type.

TRUSCOTT. I'm nervous as well. I'll be company for him—

FAY. It'd be better if I was present. He's more relaxed in the company of women.

TRUSCOTT. He'll have to come to terms with his psychological peculiarity. Out you go!

FAY *and* HAL *go off left.*

(TRUSCOTT *faces* DENNIS, *the corpse between them.*) Now then, I'm going to ask a few questions. I want sensible answers. I've had enough fooling about for one day. (*He observes* DENNIS *narrowiy.*) Have you ever been in prison?

DENNIS. Yes.

TRUSCOTT. What for?

DENNIS. Stealing overcoats and biting a policeman.

TRUSCOTT. The theft of an article of clothing is excusable. But policemen, like red squirrels, must be protected. You were rightly convicted. What do you know of paternity orders?

DENNIS. Is that when birds say you've put them in the club?

TRUSCOTT. Don't try to evade the issue. How many women have you made pregnant?

DENNIS. Five.

TRUSCOTT. You scatter your seed along the pavements without regard to age or sex. (*He taps the corpse.*) What are you doing with this? Have you taken up sewing?

DENNIS. I was putting it in the cupboard.

TRUSCOTT. Why?

DENNIS. To keep it hidden.

TRUSCOTT. Don't try to pull the wool over my eyes. I've been told the whole pathetic story. You ought to be ashamed of yourself.

DENNIS (*pause, with resignation*). Am I under arrest, then?

TRUSCOTT. I wish you were. Unfortunately what you've done isn't illegal.

DENNIS (*pause, with surprise*). When did they change the law?

TRUSCOTT. There never was any law.

DENNIS. Has it all been a leg-pull? My uncle did two years.

TRUSCOTT. What for?

DENNIS. Armed robbery.

TRUSCOTT. That is against the law.

DENNIS. It used to be.

TRUSCOTT. It still is.

DENNIS. I thought the law had been changed.

TRUSCOTT. Who told you that?

DENNIS. You did.

TRUSCOTT. When?

DENNIS. Just now. I thought there'd been a reappraisal of society's responsibilities towards the criminal.

TRUSCOTT. You talk like a judge.

DENNIS. I've met so many.

TRUSCOTT. I'm not impressed by your fine friends.

He chews on his pipe and watches DENNIS *closely.*

Where's the money from the bank job?

DENNIS. What bank job?

TRUSCOTT. Where's it buried?

DENNIS. Buried?

TRUSCOTT. Your mate says it's been buried.

DENNIS (*indignant*). He's a liar!

TRUSCOTT. A very intelligent reply. You're an honest lad. (*He smiles and puts an arm around* DENNIS'S *shoulders.*) Are you prepared to co-operate with me? I'll see you're all right.

DENNIS *edges away.*

I'll put a good word in for you.

DENNIS (*nervous, laughing to hid his embarrassment*). Can't we stand away from the window? I don't want anybody to see me talking to a policeman.

TRUSCOTT. I'm not a policeman.

DENNIS. Aren't you?

TRUSCOTT. No. I'm from the Metropolitan Water Board.

DENNIS. You're the law! You gave me a kicking down the station.

TRUSCOTT. I don't remember doing so.

DENNIS. Well, it's all in the day's work to you, isn't it?

TRUSCOTT. What were you doing down the station?

DENNIS. I was on sus.

TRUSCOTT. What were you suspected of?

DENNIS. The bank job.

TRUSCOTT. And you complain you were beaten?

DENNIS. Yes.

TRUSCOTT. Did you tell anyone?

DENNIS. Yes.

TRUSCOTT. Who?

DENNIS. The officer in charge.

TRUSCOTT. What did he say?

DENNIS. Nothing.

TRUSCOTT. Why not?

DENNIS. He was out of breath with kicking.

TRUSCOTT. I hope you're prepared to substantiate these accusations, lad. What evidence have you?

DENNIS. My bruises.

TRUSCOTT. What is the official version of those?

DENNIS. Resisting arrest.

TRUSCOTT. I can see nothing unreasonable in that. You want to watch yourself. Making unfounded allegations. You'll find yourself in serious trouble.

He takes DENNIS *by the collar and shakes him.*

If I ever hear you accuse the police of using violence on a prisoner in custody again, I'll take you down to the station and beat the eyes out of your head.

He shoves DENNIS *away.*

Now, get out!

DENNIS *is about to leave the corpse.*

And take that thing with you. I don't want to see it in here again.

DENNIS *goes off left with the corpse.*

TRUSCOTT *closes the door and, as he does so, sees something on the floor. He puts his pipe into the corner of his mouth and picks up the glass eye. He holds it to the light in order to get a better view. Puzzled. He sniffs at it. He holds it close to his ear. He rattles it. He takes out a pocket magnifying-glass and stares hard at it. He gives a brief exclamation of horror and surprise.*

Curtain

Act Two

TRUSCOTT, *by the window, is examining the eye under a pocket magnifying-glass.*

MCLEAVY *enters carrying a photograph of Pope Pius XII.* FAY *follows him.*

MCLEAVY. Is it possible to use the toilet, sir?

TRUSCOTT (*putting the eye into his pocket*). The water is off.

FAY. Who turned it off?

TRUSCOTT. My men did.

MCLEAVY (*handing the photograph to* FAY). I'm getting on the phone. I'll have your particulars filed.

TRUSCOTT. I've disconnected the telephone.

MCLEAVY. Why?

TRUSCOTT. You always begin your sentences with 'Why?' Did they teach you to at school?

MCLEAVY. Now, look here – I've a right to know – are you from the sanitary people? I never knew they had power over the post office. Aren't they separate entities? (*To* FAY.) The water board and the post office? Or have they had a merger? (*To* TRUSCOTT.) They'd never connect up the water board and the post office, would they?

TRUSCOTT. I'm not in a position to say, sir.

MCLEAVY. Produce your warrant and you're justified. If not, get out of my house. Even a Government department should take account of death.

TRUSCOTT. Less of that. I must ask you to respect my cloth.

MCLEAVY (*to* FAY). Is he a priest?

FAY. If he is he's an unfrocked one.

MCLEAVY (*stares at* TRUSCOTT, *goes closer to him, wonderingly*). Who are you?

TRUSCOTT. My name is Truscott.

MCLEAVY. What in Hell kind of a name is that? Is it an anagram? You're not bloody human, that's for sure. We're being made the victims of some kind of interplanetary rag. (*To* FAY.) He's probably luminous in the dark. (*To* TRUSCOTT.) Come on, I don't care what infernal power you represent. I want a straight answer.

> TRUSCOTT *regards* MCLEAVY *calmly and in silence.*

I'll go next door – they're Dubliners. If you're the Angel of the Lord Himself, they'll mix it with you.

TRUSCOTT. I've warned you already about leaving this room. Do as you're told or take the consequences.

MCLEAVY. I'll take the consequences.

TRUSCOTT. I can't allow you to do that.

MCLEAVY. You've no power to stop me.

TRUSCOTT. I must disagree. I'm acting under orders.

MCLEAVY. Whose?

TRUSCOTT. My superior officer's.

MCLEAVY. I don't believe he exists!

TRUSCOTT. If you don't control yourself, I shall have to caution you.

MCLEAVY. I know we're living in a country whose respect for the law is proverbial: who'd give power of arrest to the traffic lights if three women magistrates and a Liberal M.P. would only suggest it; but I've never heard of an employee of the water board nicking a kid for stealing apples, let alone a grown man for doubting whether he had any right to be on the planet.

> *Silence.* TRUSCOTT *removes his pipe from his mouth slowly, weighing his words before he speaks.*

TRUSCOTT. If you'll give me your undivided attention for a few moments, sir, I promise you we'll have this whole case sorted out. It isn't a game we're playing. It's my duty, and I must do it to the best of my ability.

The door right is flung open, DENNIS *and* HAL *burst in with the corpse.* TRUSCOTT *looks steadily and searchingly at them. He points to the corpse with his pipe.*

What are you doing with that thing?

DENNIS. We were taking it outside.

TRUSCOTT. Why? Did it need the air?

HAL. We were putting it in the garage.

TRUSCOTT. This isn't the garage. What do you mean by bringing it back into this room?

HAL. A police sergeant was in the garage.

TRUSCOTT. I'm sure he has no particular aversion to sharing a garage with a tailor's dummy.

HAL. He wanted to undress it.

TRUSCOTT. What possible objection could there be to an officer undressing a dummy?

DENNIS. It isn't decent.

HAL. It's a Catholic.

TRUSCOTT (*with contempt*). The things you say are quite ludicrous, lad. (*He laughs mirthlessly.*) Ho, ho ho. Take it to the garage. The bobby won't interfere with it. He's a married man with children.

No one moves. TRUSCOTT *chews on his pipe; he takes pipe from his mouth.*

Go on! Do as I say.

FAY. No! I'd rather it didn't go. I want it here.

TRUSCOTT. Why?

FAY. It's valuable.

TRUSCOTT. Has its value increased during the last few minutes?

FAY. No.

TRUSCOTT. If it's your usual custom to encourage young men to run up and down garden paths with tailor's dummies, you must be stopped from exercising such arbitrary power.

FAY. I did want it in the garage, but after what has been said I feel I can't allow her out of my sight.

TRUSCOTT. Really, miss, your relationship with that object verges on the criminal. Has no one in this house any normal feelings? I've never come across such people. If there's any more of it, I shall arrest the lot of you.

MCLEAVY. How does the water board go about making an arrest?

TRUSCOTT. You must have realized by now, sir, that I am not from the water board?

MCLEAVY. I have. Your behaviour was causing me grave concern.

TRUSCOTT. Any deception I practised was never intended to deceive you, sir. You are – if I may say so – an intelligent man. (*He laughs to himself.*) You saw through my disguise at once. It was merely a ruse to give me time to review the situation. To get my bearings on a very tricky assignment. Or two tricky assignments. As you will shortly realize. (*He smiles and bows to* MCLEAVY.) You have before you a man who is quite a personage in his way – Truscott of the Yard. Have you never heard of Truscott? The man who tracked down the limbless girl killer? Or was that sensation before your time?

HAL. Who would kill a limbless girl?

TRUSCOTT. She was the killer.

HAL. How did she do it if she was limbless?

TRUSCOTT. I'm not prepared to answer that question to anyone outside the profession. We don't want a carbon-copy murder on our hands. (*To* MCLEAVY.) Do you realize what I'm doing here?

MCLEAVY. No. Your every action has been a mystery to me.

TRUSCOTT. That is as it should be. The process by which the

police arrive at the solution to a mystery is, in itself, a mystery. We've reason to believe that a number of crimes have been committed under your roof. There was no legal excuse for a warrant. We had no proof. However, the water board doesn't need a warrant to enter private houses. And so I availed myself of this loophole in the law. It's for your own good that Authority behaves in this seemingly alarming way. (*With a smile.*) Does my explanation satisfy you?

MCLEAVY. Oh, yes, Inspector. You've a duty to do. My personal freedom must be sacrificed. I have no further questions.

TRUSCOTT. Good. I shall proceed to bring the crimes to light. Beginning with the least important.

HAL. What is that?

TRUSCOTT. Murder.

FAY (*anxiously*). Murder?

TRUSCOTT. Yes, murder. (*To* MCLEAVY.) Your wife passed away three days ago? What did she die of?

FAY. The death certificate is perfectly legible.

TRUSCOTT. Reading isn't an occupation we encourage among police officers. We try to keep the paper work down to a minimum. (*To* MCLEAVY.) Have you no grumble at the way your wife died?

MCLEAVY. None.

TRUSCOTT. You're easily satisfied, I see. I am not.

FAY. Mrs McLeavy 's doctor signed the death certificate.

TRUSCOTT. So I understand. But he'd just come from diagnosing a most unusual pregnancy. His mind was so occupied by the nature of the case that he omitted to take all factors into consideration and signed in a fuzz of scientific disbelief. Has anyone seen Mrs McLeavy since she died?

HAL. How could we?

TRUSCOTT. Can all of you swear you've had no commerce with the dead?

DENNIS. We're not mediums.

TRUSCOTT. That's a pity. It would have considerably simpli-
fied my task if you had been.

FAY. I wasn't going to mention it, but I had a psychic experience last night. Three parts of Mrs McLeavy materialized
to me as I was brushing my hair.

TRUSCOTT. Was her fate discussed?

FAY. Yes. In great detail.

MCLEAVY. I never knew you had visions.

TRUSCOTT (*to* FAY). Mrs McLeavy and I are perhaps the two
people most closely involved in her death. I'd be interested
to hear her on the subject.

FAY. She accused her husband of murder.

Sensation.

MCLEAVY. Me? Are you sure she accused me?

FAY. Yes.

MCLEAVY. Complete extinction has done nothing to silence her
slanderous tongue.

TRUSCOTT. Was anyone with her at the end? (*To* HAL.)
Were you?

HAL. Yes.

TRUSCOTT. Was she uneasy? Did she leave no last message?

HAL. No.

TRUSCOTT. Was this her usual custom?

HAL. She hadn't died before.

TRUSCOTT. Not to the best of your knowledge. Though I've no
doubt our information isn't as up to date as we supposed.
Did she whisper no last words? As you bent to kiss her
cheek before she expired?

HAL. She spoke of a book.

TRUSCOTT. Which?

HAL. A broken binding recurred.

TRUSCOTT. Was it a metaphor?

HAL. I took it to be so.

TRUSCOTT goes to the bookcase. He takes down a book.

TRUSCOTT. Apart from Bibles, which are notorious for broken bindings, there is this – The Trial of Phyllis McMahon. Nurse accused of murdering her patient.

He fixes FAY with a steely look; she turns pale.

One of my own cases.

He turns over pages, staring hard and with recognition at the photograph.

Look at this photograph.

HAL. It's you.

TRUSCOTT. Yes, most unflattering, isn't it? They always choose the worst. I cannot get them to print a decent picture.

He tears the photograph from the book, screws it into a ball and stuffs it into his pocket.

DENNIS. Is there a photo of the nurse?

TRUSCOTT. Unfortunately not. Someone has torn every picture of the nurse from the book.

Once again he turns his piercing gaze upon FAY; she looks uncomfortable.

However, we have something equally damning – the hand-writing of the accused.

He opens the book at a page of handwriting.

And here – (*Triumphantly he takes a sheet of paper from his pocket.*) – the evidence on which I propose to convict: a recent specimen of the handwriting of your late wife's nurse. Identical in every respect.

MCLEAVY (*staring at the sheet of paper*). But this is signed Queen Victoria.

TRUSCOTT. One of her many aliases.

> MCLEAVY *stares in amazement at the evidence.*

HAL. If it was one of your own cases, how is it she didn't recognize you?

TRUSCOTT. Two very simple reasons. I conduct my cases under an assumed voice and I am a master of disguise. (*He takes off his hat.*) You see – a complete transformation. (*To* MCLEAVY.) You've had a lucky escape, sir. You'd've been the victim of a murder bid inside a month. We've had the tabs on her for years. Thirteen fatal accidents, two cases of suspected fish poisoning. One unexplained disappearance. She's practised her own form of genocide for a decade and called it nursing.

FAY (*staring at him, agitatedly*). I never killed anyone.

TRUSCOTT. At the George V hospital in Holyhead eighty-seven people died within a week. How do you explain that?

FAY. It was the geriatric ward. They were old.

TRUSCOTT. They had a right to live, same as anybody else.

FAY. I was in the children's ward.

TRUSCOTT. How many innocents did you massacre – Phyllis?

FAY. None.

TRUSCOTT. I fail to see why you choose to cloak the episode in mystery. You can't escape.

FAY. Mrs McLeavy accused her husband.

TRUSCOTT. We can't accept the evidence of a ghost. The problems posed would be insuperable.

FAY. You must prove me guilty. That is the law.

TRUSCOTT. You know nothing of the law. I know nothing of the law. That makes us equal in the sight of the law.

FAY. I'm innocent till I'm proved guilty. This is a free country. The law is impartial.

TRUSCOTT. Who's been filling your head with that rubbish?

FAY. I can't be had for anything. You've no proof.

TRUSCOTT. When I make out my report I shall say that you've

given me a confession. It could prejudice your case if I have to forge one.

FAY. I shall deny that I've confessed.

TRUSCOTT. Perjury is a serious crime.

FAY. Have you no respect for the truth?

TRUSCOTT. We have a saying under the blue lamp 'Waste time on the truth and you'll be pounding the beat until the day you retire.'

FAY (breaking down). The British police force used to be run by men of integrity.

TRUSCOTT. That is a mistake which has been rectified. Come along now. I can't stand here all day.

FAY (drying her eyes). My name is Phyllis Jean McMahon alias Fay Jean McMahon. I am twenty-eight years of age and a nurse by profession. On the third of December last I advertised in the trade papers for a situation. Mr McLeavy answered my request. He wished me to nurse his wife back to health: a task I found impossible to perform. Mrs McLeavy was dying. Had euthanasia not been against my religion I would have practised it. Instead I decided to murder her. I administered poison during the night of June the twenty-second. In the morning I found her dead and notified the authorities. I have had nothing but heartache ever since. I am sorry for my dreadful crime. (She weeps.)

TRUSCOTT (looking up from his notebook). Very good. Your style is simple and direct. It's a theme which less skilfully handled could've given offence. (He puts away his notebook.) One of the most accomplished confessions I've heard in some time.

He gives MCLEAVY *a police whistle.*

I'll just arrange transport. Blow that if she should attempt to escape. My men will come to your aid immediately. The sooner we get a spoonful of Mrs McLeavy on a slide the sooner McMahon faces that murder rap.

He goes off left.

MCLEAVY (*to* FAY). How could you rob me of my only support?

FAY. I intended to provide a replacement.

MCLEAVY. I never knew such wickedness was possible.

FAY. You were aware of my character when you employed me. My references were signed by people of repute.

MCLEAVY. You murdered most of them.

FAY. That doesn't invalidate their signatures.

MCLEAVY. Pack your bags! You're not being arrested from my house.

FAY *dabs at her eyes with a handkerchief.*

DENNIS. I've never seen you in adversity. It's an unforgettable experience. I love you. I'll wait for you for ever.

FAY. No, you'll tire of waiting and marry someone else.

HAL. He won't be able to. (*He runs his hand along the coffin lid.*) Not when the Inspector asks to see mum's remains. He'll have us by the short hairs, baby.

TRUSCOTT *re-enters left with* MEADOWS.

TRUSCOTT. We're ready when you are, McMahon.

FAY *holds out her hand to* HAL. HAL *shakes it and kisses her.*

HAL (*kissing* FAY'S *hand*). Good-bye. I count a mother well lost to have met you.

DENNIS *kisses* FAY'S *hand.*

DENNIS. I shall write to you. We're allowed one letter a week.

FAY. How sweet you are. I'd like to take you both to prison with me.

TRUSCOTT. They'd certainly do more good in Holloway than you will. Take her away, Meadows.

MEADOWS *approaches* FAY *with the handcuffs. She holds out her hands.* MEADOWS *hesitates, bends swiftly and kisses* FAY'S *hand.*

Meadows!

MEADOWS *handcuffs* FAY, *and leads her out.*

Nothing but a miracle can save her now.

MEADOWS *goes off with* FAY.

(*To* MCLEAVY). I understand your wife is embalmed, sir?

MCLEAVY. Yes.

TRUSCOTT. It's a delicate subject, sir, but for the post-mortem we shall want Mrs McLeavy's stomach. Where are you keeping it?

MCLEAVY. In the little casket.

TRUSCOTT. Where is it?

HAL. In the hall.

TRUSCOTT. Fetch it, will you?

HAL *goes off left.*

DENNIS. I have something to say which will be a shock to you, Inspector.

TRUSCOTT (*nodding, taking out his pipe*). What is it? Tell it to your uncle (*He smiles.*)

DENNIS. After I'd reached the coffin I went back for the little casket. As I reached it a violent explosion occurred. The lid of the casket was forced open and the contents dispersed.

HAL *enters left. He carries the casket. He turns it upside down. The hinged lid swings free.*

It's well known in the trade that the viscera, when heated, is an unstable element.

HAL. The contents of my mother's stomach have been destroyed.

TRUSCOTT *shakes his head, bowled over.*

TRUSCOTT. What an amazing woman McMahon is. She's got away with it again. She must have influence with Heaven.

HAL. God is a gentleman. He prefers blondes.

TRUSCOTT. Call her back! Look sharp! She'll sue us for wrong-
ful arrest.

   HAL *and* DENNIS *go off left.*

MCLEAVY (*to* TRUSCOTT). I'm sorry, sir, but I'm rather con-
fused as to what has been said and in answer to whom.

TRUSCOTT. Briefly, sir, without your wife's stomach we have
no evidence on which to convict.

MCLEAVY. Can't you do a reconstruction job on my wife's
insides.

TRUSCOTT. Even God can't work miracles, sir.

MCLEAVY. Is the world mad? Tell me it's not.

TRUSCOTT. I'm not paid to quarrel with accepted facts.

   FAY *enters with* HAL *and* DENNIS.

Well, McMahon, you've had another twelfth-hour escape?

FAY. Yes. I shall spend a quiet hour with my rosary after tea.

MCLEAVY (*to* FAY). I know one thing, you'll be black-listed.
I'll see you never get another nursing job.

TRUSCOTT. There's no need to be vindictive. Show a little
tolerance.

MCLEAVY. Is she going to get away with murder?

TRUSCOTT. I'm afraid so, sir. However, I've an ace up my
sleeve. The situation for law and order, though difficult, is by
no means hopeless. There's still a chance, albeit a slim one,
that I can get McMahon as accessory to another crime. And
one which the law regards as far more serious than the taking
of human life.

MCLEAVY. What's more serious than mass murder?

TRUSCOTT. Stealing public money. And that is just what your
son and his accomplices have done.

MCLEAVY. Harold would never do a thing like that. He belongs
to the Sons of Divine Providence.

TRUSCOTT. That may make a difference to Divine Providence, but it cuts no ice with me.

He takes the eye from his pocket.

During the course of my investigations I came across this object. Could you explain to me what it is?

He hands the eye to MCLEAVY.

MCLEAVY (*examining it*). It's a marble.

TRUSCOTT. No. Not a marble. (*He regards* MCLEAVY *calmly.*) It looks suspiciously to me like an eye. The question I'd like answered is – to whom does it legally belong?

MCLEAVY. I'm not sure that it is an eye. I think it's a marble which has been trod on.

TRUSCOTT. It's an eye, sir. (*He takes the eye from* MCLEAVY.) The makers' name is clearly marked: J. & S. Frazer, Eye-makers to the Profession.

FAY. It's mine. My father left it to me in his will.

TRUSCOTT. That's a strange bequest for a father to make.

FAY. I always admired it. It's said to have belonged originally to a well-loved figure of the concert platform.

TRUSCOTT. You're a clever woman, McMahon. Unfortunately you're not quite clever enough. I'm no fool.

FAY. Your secret is safe with me.

TRUSCOTT. I've a shrewd suspicion where this eye came from. (*He smiles.*) You know too, don't you?

FAY. No.

TRUSCOTT. Don't lie to me! It's from your sewing dummy, isn't it?

FAY (*laughing*). It's no good, Inspector. You're too clever by half.

TRUSCOTT. I'm glad you've decided to tell the truth at last. We must return the eye to its rightful owner. Unwrap the dummy.

FAY. No, no! You can't undress her in front of four men. I must do it in private.

MCLEAVY. One moment. (*To* TRUSCOTT.) Let me see that eye.

TRUSCOTT *gives it to him.*

(*To* FAY.) Who gave you this?

FAY. It's from my dummy. Didn't you hear the Inspector?

MCLEAVY (*to* TRUSCOTT). Is it likely they'd fit eyes to a sewing machine? Does that convince you?

TRUSCOTT. Nothing ever convinces me. I choose the least unlikely explanation and file it in our records.

MCLEAVY (*to* FAY). Who gave you this? Come on now!

DENNIS. I gave it to her. A woman gave it to me as a souvenir.

MCLEAVY. Of what?

DENNIS. A special occasion.

MCLEAVY. It must've been a very special occasion if she gave you her eye to mark it. Come along, I'm not the police. I want a sensible answer. Who gave it to you?

HAL. I did.

MCLEAVY (*shrieks*). You! Oh, Sacred Heaven, no!

TRUSCOTT. We're open to serious discussion, sir, but not bad language.

MCLEAVY. This is stolen property. This eye belongs to my wife.

TRUSCOTT. On what do you base your assumption?

MCLEAVY. My wife had glass eyes.

TRUSCOTT. A remarkable woman, sir. How many were in her possession at the time of her death?

MCLEAVY. None.

TRUSCOTT. I see.

MCLEAVY. These were fitted after death. Her own were taken away.

TRUSCOTT. Where to?

MCLEAVY. I don't know.

TRUSCOTT. Did you never think to inquire?

MCLEAVY. No.

TRUSCOTT. You act in a singularly heartless manner for someone who claims to have been happily married.

MCLEAVY. Oh, Inspector – (*Brokenly*) – my son, you heard
him confess it, has stolen the eyes from the dead; a practice
unknown outside of medical science. I have reared a ghoul at
my own expense.

Silence. TRUSCOTT *considers.*

TRUSCOTT. What do you wish me to do, sir?

MCLEAVY. Fetch a screwdriver. The coffin must be opened. I
want to know what else thievery stoops to. Her head may
have gone as well.

DENNIS. Might I advise caution, Mr McLeavy? From a professional point of view? The coffin took a pasting, you know.

FAY. She may be in pieces.

MCLEAVY. Fetch a screwdriver.

HAL. Couldn't we bury the eye separately?

MCLEAVY. I can't ask the priest to hold the burial service over
an eye. Fetch a screwdriver.

Nobody moves. TRUSCOTT *draws a deep breath.*

TRUSCOTT. What good will it do, sir?

MCLEAVY. I'm not interested in doing good. There are or-
ganizations devoted to that purpose. Fetch a screwdriver!
Do I have to repeat it like the muezzin?

DENNIS *gives* MCLEAVY *a screwdriver.* MCLEAVY *hands
the eye to* TRUSCOTT *and begins to unscrew the coffin lid.*

TRUSCOTT. This is unwarranted interference with the rights of
the dead. As a policeman I must ask you to consider your
actions most carefully.

MCLEAVY. She's my wife. I can do what I like with her. Anything is legal with a corpse.

TRUSCOTT. Indeed it is not. Conjugal rights should stop with
the last heartbeat. I thought you knew that.

   MCLEAVY *begins to unscrew the second side of the coffin.*

I must say, sir, I'm aghast at this behaviour. Equivalent to
tomb robbing it is. What do you hope to gain by it? An
eyeless approach to Heaven is as likely to succeed as any.
Your priest will confirm what I say.

   MCLEAVY *bows his head, continues his work.*

You strike me, sir – I have to say this – as a thoroughly
irresponsible individual. Always creating unnecessary trouble.
HAL. We'll have the house full of the law. Half our fittings
will be missing. That's why they have such big pockets on
their uniforms.
TRUSCOTT. Your son seems to have a more balanced idea of
the world in which we live than you do, sir.
MCLEAVY. My duty is clear.
TRUSCOTT. Only the authorities can decide when your duty is
clear. Wild guesses by persons like yourself can only cause
confusion.

   MCLEAVY *lifts the coffin lid.*

HAL. He's going to be shocked. See him preparing for it. His
generation takes a delight in being outraged.

   MCLEAVY *looks into the coffin, gives a grunt of disbelief,
   staggers back, incredulous.*

DENNIS. Catch him! He's going to faint.

   He and FAY *support* MCLEAVY *and help him to the bed.*
   MCLEAVY *sinks beside the corpse in a state of shock.*

MCLEAVY. Where? (*Bewildered.*) Where? (*He follows* HAL's
glance to the corpse and recoils in horror.) Oh, the end of the
world is near when such crimes are committed.

TRUSCOTT. The opening of a coffin couldn't possibly herald Armageddon. Pull yourself together, sir.

FAY (*to* TRUSCOTT). The condition of the corpse has deteriorated due to the accident. Do you wish to verify the fact?

TRUSCOTT (*shuddering*). No, thank you, miss. I receive enough shocks in the line of duty without going about looking for them.

FAY (*to* DENNIS). Replace the lid on the coffin.

DENNIS *does so.*

MCLEAVY (*to* HAL). I shall disown you. I'll publish it abroad that I was cuckolded.

FAY (*to* TRUSCOTT). It's been a harrowing experience for him.

TRUSCOTT. He was warned in advance of the consequences of his action.

HAL (*kneeling to* MCLEAVY). I'm in a bit of a spot, Dad. I don't mind confessing. Don't get stroppy with me, eh?

MCLEAVY. I'm sorry I ever got you. I'd've withheld myself at the conception if I'd known.

TRUSCOTT. Such idle fantasies ill become you, sir.

MCLEAVY *chokes back his sobs.*

Fathers have discovered greater iniquities in their sons than the theft of an eye. The episode isn't without instruction.

MCLEAVY. Where did I go wrong? His upbringing was faultless. (*To* DENNIS.) Did you lead him astray?

DENNIS. I was innocent till I met him.

HAL. You met me when you were three days old.

MCLEAVY (*to* HAL). Where are your tears? She was your mother.

HAL. It's dust, Dad.

MCLEAVY *shakes his head in despair.*

A little dust.

MCLEAVY. I loved her.

HAL. You had her filleted without a qualm. Who could have affection for a half-empty woman?

MCLEAVY (*groaning*). Oh, Jesus, Mary, Joseph, guide me to the end of my wits and have done with it.

HAL. You've lost nothing. You began the day with a dead wife. You end it with a dead wife.

MCLEAVY. Oh, wicked, wicked. (*Wildly.*) These hairs – (*Points.*) – they're grey. You made them so. I'd be a redhead today had you been an accountant.

TRUSCOTT (*removing his pipe from his mouth*). We really can't accept such unlikely explanation for the colour of your hair, sir.

    MCLEAVY *wails aloud in anguish.*

Your behaviour indicates a growing lack of control. It's disgraceful in a man of your age and background. I'm half inclined to book you for disturbing the peace.

    FAY *hands* MCLEAVY *a handkerchief. He blows his nose. He draws himself up to his full height.*

MCLEAVY. I'm sorry, Inspector. My behaviour must seem strange to you. I'll endeavour to explain it. You can then do as you think fit.

FAY. Consider the consequences of telling the truth. It will kill Father Jellicoe.

DENNIS. My pigeons will die if I'm nicked. There'll be nobody to feed them.

    Silence. TRUSCOTT *opens his notebook and looks at* MC-LEAVY.

MCLEAVY. I wish to prefer charges.

HAL (*desperate*). If my Aunt Bridie hears of this, she'll leave her money to an orphanage. You know how selfish she is.

TRUSCOTT. Whom do you wish to charge, sir?

MCLEAVY (*pause, struggles with his conscience, at last*). Myself.

TRUSCOTT (*looking up from his notebook*). What crime have you committed?

MCLEAVY. I— I— (*Sweating.*) I've given misleading information to the police.

TRUSCOTT. What information?

MCLEAVY. I told you that the eye belonged to my wife. It doesn't. (*Conscience stricken.*) Oh, God forgive me for what I'm doing.

TRUSCOTT. If the eye doesn't belong to your wife, to whom does it belong?

> MCLEAVY *is unable to answer; he stares about him, perplexed.*

FAY (*with a smile*). It belongs to my sewing dummy, Inspector. Your original deduction was quite correct.

> TRUSCOTT *slowly puts away his notebook and pencil.*

TRUSCOTT. I ought to have my head examined, getting mixed up in a case of this kind. (*To* MCLEAVY.) Your conduct is scandalous, sir. With you for a father this lad never stood a chance. No wonder he took to robbing banks.

MCLEAVY (*in shame*). What are you going to do?

TRUSCOTT. Do? I'm going to leave this house at once. I've never come across such people. You behave as though you're affiliated to Bedlam.

MCLEAVY. But – the bank robbery – is the case closed?

TRUSCOTT. No, sir, it's not closed. We don't give up as easily as that. I'm going to have this place turned upside down.

MCLEAVY. Oh, dear, what a nuisance. And in a house of mourning, too.

TRUSCOTT. Your wife won't be here, sir. I shall take possession of the remains.

FAY. Why do you need the remains? You can't prove Mrs McLeavy was murdered.

TRUSCOTT. There's no cause for alarm. It's a mere formality.

You're quite safe. (*He smiles. To* MCLEAVY.) There's no one more touchy than your hardened criminal. (*He puts his pipe away.*) I'll be back in ten minutes. And then, I'm afraid, a lot of damage will be done to your property. You'll be paying repair bills for months to come. One unfortunate suspect recently had the roof taken off his house.

MCLEAVY. Isn't there anything I can do to prevent this appalling assault upon my privacy?

TRUSCOTT. Well, sir, if you can suggest a possible hiding-place for the money?

MCLEAVY *hangs his head.*

MCLEAVY (*almost in a whisper*). I can't, Inspector.

TRUSCOTT. Very well. You must take the consequences of ignorance. (*He tips his hat.*) I'll be back soon.

He goes off left.

MCLEAVY. Oh, what a terrible thing I've done. I've obstructed an officer in the course of his duty.

HAL (*hugging him*). I'm proud of you. I'll never feel ashamed of bringing my friends home now.

MCLEAVY. I shan't be able to face my reflection in the mirror.

FAY. Go to confession. Book an hour with Father Mac.

HAL. Oh, not him! Three brandies and he's away. The barmaid at the King of Denmark is blackmailing half the district.

MCLEAVY. I'll say nothing of what I've discovered if you return the money to the bank. You're not to keep a penny of it. Do you understand?

HAL. Yes, Dad. (*He winks at* DENNIS.)

MCLEAVY. I'll go and ring Father Jellicoe. My soul is in torment.

MCLEAVY *goes off left.*

HAL (*closing the door, to* FAY). Unwrap the body. Once we've got it back into the coffin we're home and dry.

FAY *pulls the screen round the bed. She goes behind the screen to unwrap the corpse.*

DENNIS. What are we going to do with the money?
HAL. Put in into the casket.
DENNIS. Won't he want that?
HAL. He knows it's empty.

DENNIS *takes the lid from the coffin.*

DENNIS. Why didn't we put it in there in the first place?
HAL. My mum's guts were in there. The damp would've got at the notes.

HAL *opens the casket.*

Got a hanky?

DENNIS *throws a handkerchief over.* HAL *wipes the inside of the casket.*

DENNIS. Oh, you've gone too far! Using my handkerchief for that. It was a birthday present.

HAL *throws him the handkerchief back.*

HAL. Relax, baby. You'll have other birthdays.

DENNIS *throws the bundles of notes to* HAL. HAL *packs them into the casket.*

I shall accompany my father to Confession this evening. In order to purge my soul of this afternoon's events.
DENNIS. It's at times like this that I regret not being a Catholic.
HAL. Afterwards I'll take you to a remarkable brothel I've found. Really remarkable. Run by three Pakistanis aged between ten and·fifteen. They do it for sweets. Part of their religion. Meet me at seven. Stock up with Mars bars.

FAY *appears from behind the screen, folding the mattress cover.*

FAY. Don't look behind there, Harold.

HAL. Why not?

FAY. Your mother is naked.

She hangs the folded cover over the screen.
HAL packs the last bundle of notes into the casket.

HAL. We're safe.

He bangs down the lid.

Nobody will ever look in there.

TRUSCOTT enters left.

TRUSCOTT. I've fixed everything to my satisfaction. My men will be here shortly. They're perfectly capable of causing damage unsupervised, and so I shall take my leave of you. (*He bows, smiles.*)

FAY (*shaking hands*). Good-bye, Inspector. It's been nice meeting you again.

TRUSCOTT. Good-bye. (*He nods to HAL and DENNIS.*) I'd better take the little casket with me.

HAL. It's empty!

TRUSCOTT. I must have it certified empty before I close my report.

FAY. We're having it de-sanctified. Mr McLeavy is on the phone to the priest about it.

TRUSCOTT. Our lads in forensic aren't interested in sanctity. Give me that casket!

MCLEAVY enters left. He sees TRUSCOTT and cowers back.

MCLEAVY. You're back already? Have you decided to arrest me after all?

TRUSCOTT. I wouldn't arrest you if you were the last man on earth. (*To HAL.*) Give me that casket! (*He takes the casket from HAL. To MCLEAVY.*) I'll give you a receipt, sir.

He looks for somewhere to rest the casket, sees the empty coffin puts the casket down.

Where is Mrs McLeavy?

FAY. She's behind the screen.

TRUSCOTT *looks behind the screen and raises his eyebrows.*

TRUSCOTT. Did she ask to be buried like that?

MCLEAVY. Yes.

TRUSCOTT. She was a believer in that sort of thing?

MCLEAVY. Yes.

TRUSCOTT. Are you, sir?

MCLEAVY. Well no. I'm not a member myself.

TRUSCOTT. A member? She belonged to a group, then?

MCLEAVY. Oh, yes. They met a couple of times a week. They do a lot of good for the country. Raising money for charities, holding fetes. The old folk would be lost without them.

TRUSCOTT. I've heard many excuses for nudists, sir, but never that one.

MCLEAVY (*pause*). Nudists?

TRUSCOTT. Your wife was a nudist, you say?

MCLEAVY. My wife never took her clothes off in public in her life.

TRUSCOTT. Yet she asked to be buried in that condition?

MCLEAVY. What condition?

TRUSCOTT. In the nude.

MCLEAVY (*with dignity*). You'd better leave my house, Inspector. I can't allow you to insult the memory of my late wife.

TRUSCOTT (*tearing a sheet of paper from his notebook*). You give me a lot of aggravation, sir. Really you do. (*He hands the paper to* MCLEAVY.) You'll get your property back in due course.

He lifts casket, the lid swings away and the bundles of bank-notes fall to the floor. TRUSCOTT *stares at the notes scattered at his feet in silence.*

Who is responsible for this disgraceful state of affairs?

HAL. I am.

TRUSCOTT (*stoops and picks up a bundle of notes*). Would you have stood by and allowed this money to be buried in holy ground?

HAL. Yes.

TRUSCOTT. How dare you involve me in a situation for which no memo has been issued. (*He turns the notes over.*) In all my experience I've never come across a case like it. Every one of these fivers bears a portrait of the Queen. It's dreadful to contemplate the issues raised. Twenty thousand tiaras and twenty thousand smiles buried alive! She's a constitutional monarch, you know. She can't answer back.

DENNIS. Will she send us a telegram?

TRUSCOTT. I'm sure she will.

He picks up another bundle and stares at them.

MCLEAVY. Well, Inspector, you've found the money and unmasked the criminals. You must do your duty and arrest them. I shall do mine and appear as witness for the prosecution.

HAL. Are you married, Inspector?

TRUSCOTT. Yes.

HAL. Does your wife never yearn for excitement?

TRUSCOTT. She did once express a wish to see the windmills and tulip fields of Holland.

HAL. With such an intelligent wife you need a larger income.

TRUSCOTT. I never said my wife was intelligent.

HAL. Then she's unintelligent? Is that it?

TRUSCOTT. My wife is a woman. Intelligence doesn't really enter into the matter.

HAL. If, as you claim, your wife is a woman, you certainly need a larger income.

TRUSCOTT *takes his pipe from his pocket and sticks it into the corner of his mouth.*

TRUSCOTT. Where is this Jesuitical twittering leading us?

HAL. I'm about to suggest bribery.

    TRUSCOTT removes his pipe, no one speaks.

TRUSCOTT. How much?

HAL. Twenty per cent.

TRUSCOTT. Twenty-five per cent. Or a full report of this case appears on my superior officer's desk in the morning.

HAL. Twenty-five it is.

TRUSCOTT (*shaking hands*). Done.

DENNIS (*to* TRUSCOTT). May I help you to replace the money in the casket?

TRUSCOTT. Thank you, lad. Most kind of you.

    DENNIS packs the money into the casket. FAY takes MRS MCLEAVY'S clothes from the bedpan on the invalid chair and goes behind the screen. TRUSCOTT chews on his pipe. HAL and DENNIS take the coffin behind the screen.

MCLEAVY. Has no one considered my feelings in all this?

TRUSCOTT. What percentage do you want?

MCLEAVY. I don't want money. I'm an honest man.

TRUSCOTT. You'll have to mend your ways then.

MCLEAVY. I shall denounce the lot of you!

TRUSCOTT. Now then, sir, be reasonable. What has just taken place is perfectly scandalous and had better go no farther than these three walls. It's not expedient for the general public to have its confidence in the police force undermined. You'd be doing the community a grave disservice by revealing the full frighening facts of this case.

MCLEAVY. What kind of talk is that? You don't make sense.

TRUSCOTT. Who does?

MCLEAVY. I'll go to the priest. He makes sense. He makes sense to me.

TRUSCOTT. Does he make sense to himself? That is much more important.

MCLEAVY. If I can't trust the police, I can still rely on the Fathers. They'll advise me what to do!

He goes off left. HAL *appears from behind the screen.*

HAL. You'll be glad to know that my mother is back in her last resting-place.

TRUSCOTT. Good. You've carried out the operation with speed and efficiency. I congratulate you.

DENNIS appears from behind the screen.

DENNIS. We're ready for the eye now. If you'd like to assist us.

TRUSCOTT (*taking the eye from his pocket*). You do it, lad. You're more experienced in these matters than me.

He hands DENNIS *the eye.*

HAL. You'd better have these as well.

He hands DENNIS *the teeth.*
DENNIS *takes the eye and teeth behind the screen.*

TRUSCOTT. Your sense of detachment is terrifying, lad. Most people would at least flinch upon seeing their mother's eyes and teeth handed around like nuts at Christmas.

FAY appears from behind the screen.

FAY. Have you given a thought to the priest?

TRUSCOTT. We can't have him in on it, miss. Our percentage wouldn't be worth having.

FAY. Mr McLeavy has threatened to expose us.

TRUSCOTT. I've been exposed before.

FAY. What happened?

TRUSCOTT. I arrested the man. He's doing twelve years.

HAL. If you wish to arrest my dad, you'll find me an exemplary witness.

TRUSCOTT. What a bright idea. We've vacancies in the force for lads of your calibre. (*To* FAY.) Are you with us, McMahon?

FAY. Yes, it seems the best solution for all of us.

DENNIS folds up the screen. The coffin is lying on the bed.

TRUSCOTT (*to* DENNIS). And you?

DENNIS. I've never seen the view from the witness box. It'll be a new experience.

The door left bursts open. MCLEAVY *enters with* MEADOWS.

MCLEAVY (*pointing to* TRUSCOTT). This is the man. Arrest him.

TRUSCOTT. Good afternoon, Meadows. Why have you left your post?

MEADOWS. I was accosted by this man, sir. He insisted that I accompany him to the Catholic church.

TRUSCOTT. What did you say?

MEADOWS. I refused.

TRUSCOTT. Quite rightly. You're a Methodist. Proceed with the statement.

MEADOWS. The man became offensive, sir. He made a number of derogatory remarks about the force in general and yourself in particular. I called for assistance.

TRUSCOTT. Excellent, Meadows. I shall see H.Q. hear of this. You have apprehended, in full flight, a most dangerous criminal. As you know, we've had our eye upon this house for some time. I was about to unmask the chief offender when this man left the room on some excuse and disappeared.

MEADOWS. He was making a bolt for it, sir.

TRUSCOTT. You have the matter in a nutshell, Meadows. Put the cuffs on him.

MEADOWS handcuffs MCLEAVY.

You're fucking nicked, my old beauty. You've found to your cost that the standards of the British police force are as high as ever.

MCLEAVY. What am I charged with?

TRUSCOTT. That needn't concern you for the moment. We'll fill in the details later.

MCLEAVY. You can't do this. I've always been a law-abiding citizen. The police are for the protection of ordinary people.

TRUSCOTT. I don't know where you pick up these slogans, sir. You must read them on hoardings.

MCLEAVY. I want to see someone in authority.

TRUSCOTT. I am in authority. You can see me.

MCLEAVY. Someone higher.

TRUSCOTT. You can see whoever you like, providing you convince me first that you're justified in seeing them.

MCLEAVY. You're mad!

TRUSCOTT. Nonsense. I had a check-up only yesterday. Our medical officer assured me that I was quite sane.

MCLEAVY. I'm innocent. (*A little unsure of himself, the beginnings of panic.*) Doesn't that mean anything to you?

TRUSCOTT. You know the drill, Meadows. Empty his pockets and book him.

MCLEAVY *is dragged away by* MEADOWS.

MCLEAVY. I'm innocent! I'm innocent! (*At the door, pause, a last wail.*) Oh, what a terrible thing to happen to a man who's been kissed by the Pope.

MEADOWS *goes off with* MCLEAVY.

DENNIS. What will you charge him with, Inspector?

TRUSCOTT. Oh, anything will do.

FAY. Can an accidental death be arranged?

TRUSCOTT. Anything can be arranged in prison.

HAL. Except pregnancy.

TRUSCOTT. Well, of course, the chaperon system defeats us there.

He picks up the casket.

The safest place for this is in my locker at the station. It's a maxim of the force: 'Never search your own backyard – you may find what you're looking for.' (*He turns in the doorway, the casket under his arm.*) Give me a ring this evening. I should have news for you of McLeavy by then. (*He hands a card to* FAY.) This is my home address. I'm well known there.

He nods, smiles, and goes off left. Sound of front door slamming. Pause.

HAL (*with a sigh*). He's a nice man. Self-effacing in his way.

DENNIS. He has an open mind. In direct contrast to the usual run of civil servant.

HAL and DENNIS lift the coffin from the bed and place it on the trestles.

HAL. It's comforting to know that the police can still be relied upon when we're in trouble.

They stand beside the coffin, FAY *in the middle.*

FAY. We'll bury your father with your mother. That will be nice for him, won't it?

She lifts her rosary and bows her head in prayer.

HAL (*pause, to* DENNIS). You can kip here, baby. Plenty of room now. Bring your bags over tonight.

FAY *looks up.*

FAY (*sharply*). When Dennis and I are married we'd have to move out.

HAL. Why?

FAY. People would talk. We must keep up appearances.

She returns to her prayers, her lips move silently. DENNIS *and* HAL *at either side of the coffin.*

Curtain

Author's Note

to the first edition of the play in 1967

The Lord Chamberlain grants a licence to the play subject to the following conditions:

(i) The corpse is inanimate and not played by an actress.

(ii) On page 79 the casket is wiped with a handkerchief. The Lord Chamberlain is particularly anxious that no stain shall appear on the handkerchief.

The following alterations to the text are required:

Act One: Page 21 'Run by a woman who was connected with the Royal Family one time.' For 'Royal Family' substitute 'Empire Loyalists'.

Page 22 'Under that picture of the Sacred Heart.' For 'Sacred Heart' substitute 'Infant Samuel'.

Page 36 'While Jesus pointed to his Sacred Heart, you pointed to yours. I never point. It's rude' must be cut.

Page 39 For 'Consummatum Est' substitute 'Kingdom Come'.

Page 51 For 'buggery' substitute 'beggary'.

Act Two: Page 79 'Run by three Pakistanis aged between ten and fifteen. They do it for sweets. Part of their religion.' For 'Pakistanis' substitute 'kids'. 'Part of their religion' must be cut.

Page 85 For 'fucking' substitute 'bleeding'.

Notes

[These notes are intended for use by overseas students as well as by English-born readers. Orton makes considerable use in the play of slang and colloquial language. Where a term of this type is explained in the notes the abbreviation (coll.) is used.]

6   In the lines preceding this epigraph taken from Shaw's *Misalliance* (1914) Lord Summerhays has just explained to Gunner how, in the days when Summerhays was a colonial provincial governor, he would have dealt with an agitator who threatened the established order. He would have ordered a policeman to provoke the troublesome individual into 'obstructing an officer in the discharge of his duty'. The agitator could then 'be charged and imprisoned until things quieted down'.

Act One

7   *Leeds* — city in West Yorkshire, a centre of the clothing and textiles industry.

8   *the Society* — organization, probably a Catholic foundation, which supervises the allocation of nurses to the sick.

8   *with flying colours* — with triumphant success.

8   *Benedictine monk* — member of the monastic order established by St. Benedict around 540 A.D.

9   *the League of Mary* — (or Legion of Mary), established by the Roman Catholic Church for the sanctification of its members, men and women, by prayer and active apostolic work.

9   *St Kilda's* — McLeavy's local Catholic church (see page 11).

9   *The Fraternity of the Little Sisters* — religious order of the Catholic church, spread over thirty countries, with special responsibility for the care of the aged.

9   *The Holy Father* — the Pope, the head of the Catholic church. (Orton is satirising here the dependence of Catholics on the infallible pronouncements of the Pope on all matters of faith and belief.)

9   *free thinker* — rationalist, person who, especially in religious matters, rejects authority and comes to his own opinions independently.

9 *thorn in my flesh* — source of constant irritation.

9 *Papal dispensation* — authorization granted by the Pope which provides exemption from a rule of church law. (Fay is exaggerating somewhat here, but she is referring to the Catholic church's proscription of all forms of artificial contraception.)

10 *knight of the Order of St Gregory* — a papal honour.

11 *If she'd played her cards right . . . as co-respondent* — i.e. if Mrs. McLeavy had made the most of her chances she might have used her husband's obsessive interest in roses as sufficient grounds for divorce.

11 *The Vatican* — the papal authority.

11 *the egg* — refers to the custom of giving chocolate eggs as presents at Easter.

11 *slot machines* — machines operated by inserting a coin and used for gambling or for dispensing small articles such as chocolate or cigarettes.

12 *the Fathers* — priests.

12 *not even a baby* — i.e. an illegitimate pregnancy or birth.

13 *The Friends of Bingo* — social club attached to the local church which meets to play bingo, a gambling game played by covering up numbers on a card as the numbers are called out by the person running the game. The 'large wreath marked off into numbered squares' is a representation, in somewhat bad taste, of the kind of card used to play bingo.

14 *The playground of international crime* — a journalistic cliché for a place where criminals from all round the world can live in luxury off the fruits of their crimes while being safe from arrest.

14 *You'll have to get up early in the morning to catch me* — you will have to be extremely quick-witted to outwit me. (coll.)

14 *Catholic Truth Society* — organization of members of the Roman Catholic Church, the aims of which are to spread information about their faith by means of the publication and distribution of pamphlets and books.

14 *set your adrenalin flowing* — stimulate you into a pleasing state of excitement.

14 *Penzance* — westernmost town in England, holiday resort and fishing port situated in south-west Cornwall.

15 *floral tributes* — wreaths and flowers sent by mourners as a mark of condolence at a funeral.

15 *too near the grave* — too close to death, decrepit.

16   *W.V.S.* — Women's Voluntary Service (now W.R.V.S.), organization which performs various charitable services.

17   *steep* — unduly expensive (coll.)

17   *Chapel of Rest* — that part of the undertaker's premises where relatives and friends of the deceased may view the body after it has been prepared for burial.

17   *It's terrible thoughts that come to me* — an Irish idiom of speech.

17   *by any lights* — according to any reasonable opinion or judgement. (coll.)

18   *hamstrung by red tape* — prevented from carrying out their duties effectively by obstructive official regulations and bureaucratic procedure.

18   *lift my hat to you* — give you my full admiration, congratulate you. (coll.)

18   *batten down the hatches* — screw down the lid of the coffin. (An irreverent term in this context — usually it refers to the nailing of a strip of wood over the tarpaulin of a ship's hatch to make it secure.)

18   *the law* — policemen.

18   *Knocked us up* — woke us up, got us out of bed. (coll.)

18   *swore blind* — declared in the strongest terms. (coll.)

19   *nicked* — arrested, put in prison. (coll.)

19   *spade* — negro. (offensive slang)

19   *comics* — children's magazine containing comic strips and cartoons.

21   *Freudian nightmare* — liable to arouse an unhealthy and grotesque sexual trauma. (One of the most famous theories of Sigmund Freud (1865-1939), the Austrian founder of psychoanalysis, was his concept of the Oedipus complex which affirms that sons from an early age develop a largely unconscious sexual attachment to their mothers.)

21   *unforgivable sin* — a mortal sin, regarded by Catholics as leading to total loss of grace, spiritual death.

21   *bird* — young woman. (coll.)

21   *crumpet* — sexually desirable women. (coll.)

21   *I'm on the wagon . . . to marry* — i.e. I am abstaining from sex (usually 'being on the wagon' refers to giving up alcoholic drink) so that the concentration of repressed passion will act as a stimulus to getting married. (coll.)

22   *Papal nuncio* — Pope's diplomatic representative, ambassador. (Here standing for what Hal takes to be sexual frigidity.)

22   *do it* — have sexual intercourse. (coll.)

22   *Knocked it off* — had sex with her. (obscene slang)

22   *picture of the Sacred Heart* — used by Catholics as a devotional aid, a picture representing the heart of Christ, usually shown as bleeding, which symbolizes His sacrificial love.

22   *living for kicks* — seeking constant and immediate stimulus, living for the pleasure of the moment. (coll.)

22   *stretch* — period of imprisonment, prison sentence. (coll.)

22   *Borstal* — prison-type institution in which corrective training is administered to young delinquents, aged 15-21.

22   *rabbit punch* — sharp blow delivered with the back of the hand.

22   *cobblers* — testicles. (obscene slang)

22   *'strewth* — mild oath (literally, 'God's truth') expressing distress.

22   *old lady* — mother. (coll.)

23   *sanitary people* — council department concerned with public health (water supply, sewage disposal etc.).

23   *warrant* — authorization, issued by a justice of the peace, allowing the police to enter and search premises.

23   *embroidered text* — verses from the Bible worked into cloth in a decorative style of needlework.

24   *water board* — see note on 'sanitary people', page 23.

25   *make it worth his while* — ensure he was suitably treated or rewarded.

25   *King of Denmark* — name of public house (pub).

26   *spell* — indicate.

26   *Battle of Mons* — Mons, a town in Belgium near the French border, was a battleground in both world wars, though the reference here is probably to the first battle fought against the Germans in 1914 by the British Expeditionary Force.

26   *Sadler's Wells* — theatre in Islington, London, particularly associated with ballet and opera. The Sadler's Wells Ballet Company has been known as The Royal Ballet since 1957.

27   *the daily bread* — the everyday occurrences, characteristic episodes.

29   *a stone's throw* — very short distance.

29   *Father Jellicoe* — priest at McLeavy's local Catholic church (see page 46).

29   *proven* — legally validated, established as genuine.

30   *bonds* — documents issued by a government or public

company promising the repayment with interest of borrowed
money.

31 *traditional positions* — in a conventional proposal of marriage
the man is supposed to kneel. There is also a sexual innuendo here.

31 *abstract nouns* — words which denote not concrete things
but qualities or states of mind — eg. love, devotion.

31 *Mother's Union* — social organization for married women,
attached to a local church.

32 *effing and blinding* — swearing and uttering obscenities. (coll.)

32 *pay my addresses* — make a formal proposal of marriage.

33 *The income from fairgrounds . . .* — i.e. Fay is sardonically
suggesting that she might earn some money from displaying Hal
(with his two moustaches) as a freak in a sideshow at a fair. This is
followed by a sexual innuendo.

34 *black-edged handkerchiefs* — traditionally carried by
mourners at a funeral.

34 *coatee* — a short coat.

35 *The money is putting on . . . still waiting* — Hal's reworking
of a verse from the fifteenth chapter of St. Paul's First Epistle to
the Corinthians which is used in the funeral service: '. . . the
dead shall be raised incorruptible, and we shall be changed. For this
corruptible must put on incorruption, and this mortal must put on
immortality.' (Hal means that it is the loot that is being interred
while the corpse itself still awaits burial.)

35 *make it to the altar* — manage to get married (to McLeavy).

35 *done you* — had sex with you. (obscene slang)

36 *While Jesus pointed to his Sacred Heart* — see note on
'picture of the Sacred Heart', page 22.

36 *grass* — turn informer, provide the police with information.
(coll.)

36 *Burke and Hare* — two notorious early nineteenth-century
body-snatchers (and murderers) who sold corpses to Edinburgh
anatomists.

36 *back-seat driver* — passenger in car who directs a stream of
unwanted advice at the driver.

38 *two-star* — Hal is imagining that brothels might be given a
star rating, as is the case with hotels and restaurants, according
to the standard of the facilities and service they offer.

38 *'By Appointment'. Like jam* — products (such as jam) which
are used by the Royal Family may be given the monarch's seal
of approval; this enables the manufacturer to indicate on the
product that it has received royal patronage.

38   *colour bar* — racial discrimination.

38   *kip* — sleep. (coll.)

39   *the Consummatum Est* — the name for the brothel
blasphemously adopts (from the Latin Vulgate Bible) Christ's
words on the cross just before he died: 'It is finished'. There is also
an innuendo here on the idea of sexual consummation.

39   *house of ill-fame* — brothel.

39   *National Health* — the national system of subsidized medical
care provides dentures which may be inferior to those bought
privately.

39   *at the table* — gambling. (Usually the phrase refers to more
glamorous forms of gambling than Mrs McLeavy's indulgence in
bingo — see note to page 13.)

40   *The dead can't bury themselves* — compare Christ's
injunction to the man who wished to go and bury his father
(*Mat* 8, 22 & *Luke* 9, 60).

40   *search warrant* — see note to page 23.

41   *fool's errand* — a fruitless task, an intentionally false trail.

41   *fait accompli* — something already done; an established fact
no longer worth arguing against. (French)

42   *rhumba* — ballroom dance (of Cuban origin) which requires
fairly vigorous and rhythmical bodily movements.

42   *in their pockets* — under their control, on their side. (coll.)

43   *bobby* — policeman. (coll.)

43   *a Pharaoh* — i.e. the embalmed body of an Ancient Egyptian
king, a mummy. (This leads to a pun on 'mummy' which is also a
child's word for mother.)

43   *take the mickey* — attempt to make fun of, tease in a
mocking or annoying way. (coll.)

43   *literal-minded* — inclined to take things at their face value or
matter-of-fact level.

46   *S.J.* — member of the Society of Jesus, a Roman Catholic
religious order.

46   *piss-taking* — attempts to mock, make a fool of somebody.
(crude slang)

48   *quoting St Paul* — see note to page 35.

48   *Highway code* — booklet issued by the Department of
Transport for the guidance of drivers and other road users. (The
contrast with St. Paul is intended by Truscott to be dismissively
bathetic.)

48   *chlorinate* — literally means to treat with chlorine, a toxic
substance used in the purification of water and as a disinfectant.

The essence of Truscott's threat, therefore, seems to involve the idea of washing down some infected object (Hal) with a strong cleansing agent.

48   *You'll be laughing . . . bloody face* — You will soon be made to feel quite the reverse of your attempts to have fun at my expense; I'll turn your laughter into tears. (coll.)

49   *Are you qualified?* — Do you have the authority, the legal power (to make such a report)?

50   *Afghan hound* — breed of large, silky-coated hunting and sheep dog, originating from Afghanistan and northern India; kept as a pet in Europe.

51   *blown to buggery* — totally destroyed. (offensive slang)

51   *replay* — re-arranged date for the funeral. (More usually the word is used in connection with a return football match after a draw in a cup competition.)

51   *Madonna* — picture or statue of the Virgin Mary.

51   *lying in state* — formal, ceremonious display of the body of an important personage so that the corpse may be placed on public view before burial.

51   *His Holiness* — the Pope.

53   *Formaldehyde* — can used by morticians as a disinfectant and preservative.

54   *M.P.* — Member of Parliament. A constituent may raise with his elected member of parliament any issue which concerns his own rights or beliefs.

54   *Our Lady's Festival* — Our Lady is the title given to the Virgin Mary whom Catholics regard, with Christ, as the co-redeemer of mankind. The reference here may be to Lady day (originally Our Lady day), 25 March, the Feast of the Annunciation.

54   *appliance* — McLeavy's stab at the word 'appliance'.

56   *red squirrels* — the native red squirrel is being displaced rapidly in Britain by the grey squirrel.

56   *paternity order* — court order requiring the father of an illegitimate child to contribute regularly a set sum of money to assist the mother in the care of the child.

56   *put them in the club* — make them pregnant. (coll.)

56   *You scatter your seed along the pavements* — you indulge widely in promiscuous sex (recalling Dryden's reference in *Absalom and Achitophel* to Charles II who 'wide as his command,/ Scatter'd his Maker's image through the land').

56   *pull the wool over my eyes* — deceive, hoodwink me.

56   *leg-pull* — practical joke, a piece of playful deception. (coll.)
56   *did two years* — served a prison sentence of two years. (coll.)
57   *I'll see you're all right* — I'll make sure that you don't come to any harm, that your interests are well-served. (coll.)
57   *on sus* — on suspicion, as a possible suspect. (coll.)

Act Two
59   *Pope Pius XII* — Eugenio Pacelli (1876-1958), Pope (1939-58). His stance towards the Axis powers during the Second World War has been the source of some controversy.
59   *respect my cloth* — show the proper deference to my calling, profession. ('Cloth' usually refers specifically to members of the clergy.)
59   *unfrocked* — (in the case of a priest) deprived of his ecclesiastical status, usually for some serious misconduct.
60   *interplanetary rag* — practical joke on a huge, cosmic scale.
60   *mix it* — fight it out in a roughhouse style, give as good as they get. (coll.)
60   *caution* — issue a formal warning (given by a policeman to somebody suspected or accused of a crime) that his words may be taken down and used in evidence.
60   *nicking* — arresting. (coll.)
62   *the Yard* — Scotland Yard, headquarters of the police force of metropolitan London and noted particularly for its Criminal Investigation Department (CID).
62   *carbon-copy murder* — a second identical murder committed by someone who was motivated to emulate the original crime by learning all the details about it.
63   *paper work* — clerical work such as filling in forms or completing reports.
63   *a fuzz* — stupefied state of mind, a daze.
66   *We've had the tabs on her* — we've had her under close observation.
66   *Holyhead* — largest town of Anglesey, an island off the north-west coast of Wales; provides a ferry service to the Irish Republic.
67   *under the blue lamp* — in the police force. (A blue lamp over the entrance was formerly the distinguishing mark of many police stations.)
67   *trade papers* — professional journals, magazines (in this case for nursing) in which job vacancies would be advertised.
67   *a spoonful . . . on the slide* — biological specimens that are

to be examined under a microscope are first mounted on a small glass plate (a slide). Truscott wishes to establish the cause of Mrs McLeavy's death.

67 *murder rap* — murder charge. (slang characteristic of American detective stories and films)

68 *by the short hairs* — totally at his mercy. (coll.)

68 *Holloway* — prison for women in north London.

69 *Tell it to your uncle* — spoken in a coaxing, apparently ingratiating tone; it means something like 'You can confide in me, someone you trust, can't you?' (coll.)

70 *God is a gentleman. He prefers blondes* — a reworking of the title of the novel by Anita Loos, *Gentlemen Prefer Blondes* (1925).

70 *twelfth-hour* — achieved at the latest possible time.

70 *an ace up my sleeve* — effective way of gaining the advantage which is kept in reserve.

70 *one which the law regards . . . human life* — probably a reference to the Great Train Robbery (8 August, 1963) in which £2,500,000 was stolen from the Glasgow to London night mail train. The thirty year prison sentences which were given to the principal robbers led to some widely publicized indignation over the fact that theft, albeit of a staggeringly high sum of money, should rate a far more severe punishment than that normally meted out by the courts for murder.

70 *Sons of Divine Providence* — religious order of the Catholic church which runs colleges, worker hostels, hospitals and homes for the sick, infirm and handicapped. (As with other examples of the introduction into the play of names of this kind from the Catholic church, Orton seems attracted more by the absurd possibilities inherent in the name than with its precise reference.)

71 *cuts no ice with me* — does not impress me. (coll.)

71 *marble* — small glass ball used in children's games.

73 *a pasting* — severe battering. (coll.)

73 *muezzin* — Mohammedan official who calls the faithful to prayer five times a day from the balcony of one of the towers of a mosque.

74 *conjugal rights* — sexual relations between husband and wife.

75 *Armageddon* — the end of the world. (The name given in *Revelations* xvi, 16 to the place of the final catastrophic battle between the kings of the earth.)

75 *I was cuckolded* — my wife committed adultery (and therefore my son is not my own flesh and blood).

75 *stroppy* — awkward, difficult to deal with. (coll.)

75   *got you* – conceived you.

75   *withheld myself* – practised *coitus interruptus*.

76   *filleted* – literally, to cut flesh from the bone into narrow slices.(Hal is thinking of the mortician's embalming of the corpse.)

76   *had you been an accountant* – i.e. if you had followed soberly any worthy, respectable profession.

76   *book* – charge, make a formal accusation (of a crime).

77   *Bedlam* – the madhouse, lunatic asylum. (Originally the popular name for the Hospital of St. Mary of Bethlehem, a home for the insane in London.)

78   *Three brandies and he's away* – i.e. even after a relatively small amount of alcohol his tongue is loosened and he gossips about the secrets of the confessional.

79   *Mars bars* – brand name of a chocolate bar.

80   *forensic* – department concerned with applying medical knowledge (to determine such matters as the cause of death) in order to supply evidence for a court case.

82   *memo* – memorandum, a document which sets out the routine and established procedures which are to be followed by members of an organization.

82   *She can't answer back* – this rather hackneyed term is often directed at those who criticize the monarch; it is meant to remind them of the unfairness of their attacks as convention forbids the sovereign the right of reply in such cases.

82   *send us a telegram* – a reference to the monarch's marking of some notable achievement by a subject (includes attaining the age of a hundred) by the sending of a congratulatory telegram.

83   *Jesuitical twittering* – indirect, impenetrable chatter.

83   *three walls* – the usual phrase is 'no father than these four walls', which means that the subject under discussion must not be disclosed to anybody not present; here the 'fourth wall' is beyond the proscenium arch – i.e. the audience.

85   *Methodist* – member of one of the Nonconformist churches following the system of Christian belief expounded by John Wesley.

85   *H.Q.* – headquarters.

85   *my old beauty* – normally a term expressing affection, though chiefly indicative here of Truscott's mood of carefree triumph. (See John Lahr's biography of Orton – Penguin edition, pages 236-7 – for an interesting sidelight on this line.)

86   *chaperon system* – requiring the supervision of prisoners during visits by a member of the same sex.

87   *civil servant* — used here in the broadest sense of someone
(eg. a policeman) working in the public service of the state.

88   *Author's Note* — see Introduction, page xviii.

Questions for further study

1. To what extent and with what degree of success does *Loot* make a virtue of bad taste?
2. 'The play's final line about "keeping up appearances" would suggest that the main target of *Loot* is native hypocrisy when it comes to dealing with the "unmentionable" sides of British life.' To what extent would you agree?
3. Given that Fay is the only female character in *Loot*, what light does her depiction throw on Orton's view of women?
4. Orton declared that *Loot* needed to be acted with absolute realism because everything the characters say is true. To what extent does the significance of this particular farce rely on its being played 'straight'?
5. 'If "bedroom farce" tends to focus on the eccentricities and inanities of human sexual behaviour when governed by what is uncontrollable, Orton seems to find what might be called "deathroom farce" a more appropriate term to describe what is unavoidable and inevitable.' Comment on *Loot*'s treatment of death in the light of this observation.
6. What is the significance of McLeavey's role in *Loot*?
7. 'In *Loot*, Orton introduced into the garden of innocence of traditional British farce a forbidden fruit derived from the Theatre of the Absurd and from black comedy.' Consider the implications of this observation as it affects an interpretation of the play.
8. In another context, the German playwright Bertolt Brecht spoke of the 'horror' at the heart of farce. How appropriate is this for *Loot*?
9. '*Loot* appears to resemble a patchwork of sophisticated parodies.' Consider Orton's handling of genres such as the whodunnit and the comedy of manners within the play in the light of this comment.
10. In what ways and with what degree of success does Orton exploit the character of Truscott to expose the venality and stupidity of the police and the violent arbitrariness of

institutional authority?

11. Critics complain about an absence of human feeling in *Loot*. If this is the case what are we to make of those stage directions in the play which describe 'pain', 'shock', 'inner struggle', 'contempt', 'bafflement', 'fury', 'horror and surprise', etc.?

12. *A Mad World My Masters* (Thomas Middleton, dramatist, 1570–1627): how appropriate an alternative title for *Loot* might this be?

13. 'Orton likes to create an amusing incongruity between elements of stylisation in his dialogue and the outlandish or morally squalid subject matter it transmits.' Discuss.

14. 'There is a hard political centre to *Loot* which achieves a subversive effect far removed from mere anarchy.' To what extent do you agree?

15. Truscott: 'What has taken place is perfectly scandalous and had better go no farther than these three walls.' Comment on Orton's deployment of self-conscious theatricality and theatrical cliché in *Loot* and consider its significance.

16. Comment on Orton's handing of 'the sacred' and 'the profane' in *Loot*.

17. Dramatic structure is an important ingredient in farce. Discuss Orton's use of the stage – especially his timing of events and his simultaneous juxtaposition of moments of on-stage action.

18. To what extent does the comic language of *Loot* rely on an audience's recognition of banal aphorism, literary pastiche, sententiousness, chopped logic, non-sequitur, hyperbole and double entendre?

19. Consider Orton's debt to Oscar Wilde in *Loot*, especially its echoes of *The Importance of Being Earnest*.

20. Orton is said to have been influenced by seventeenth-century Restoration comedy, which in turn was embued with the philosophy of Thomas Hobbes, who famously characterised human life as 'nasty, brutish and short'. Discuss this, with particular reference to the world which *Loot* describes, or by comparing *Loot* with Etherege's *The Man of Mode* or Wycherley's *The Country Wife*.